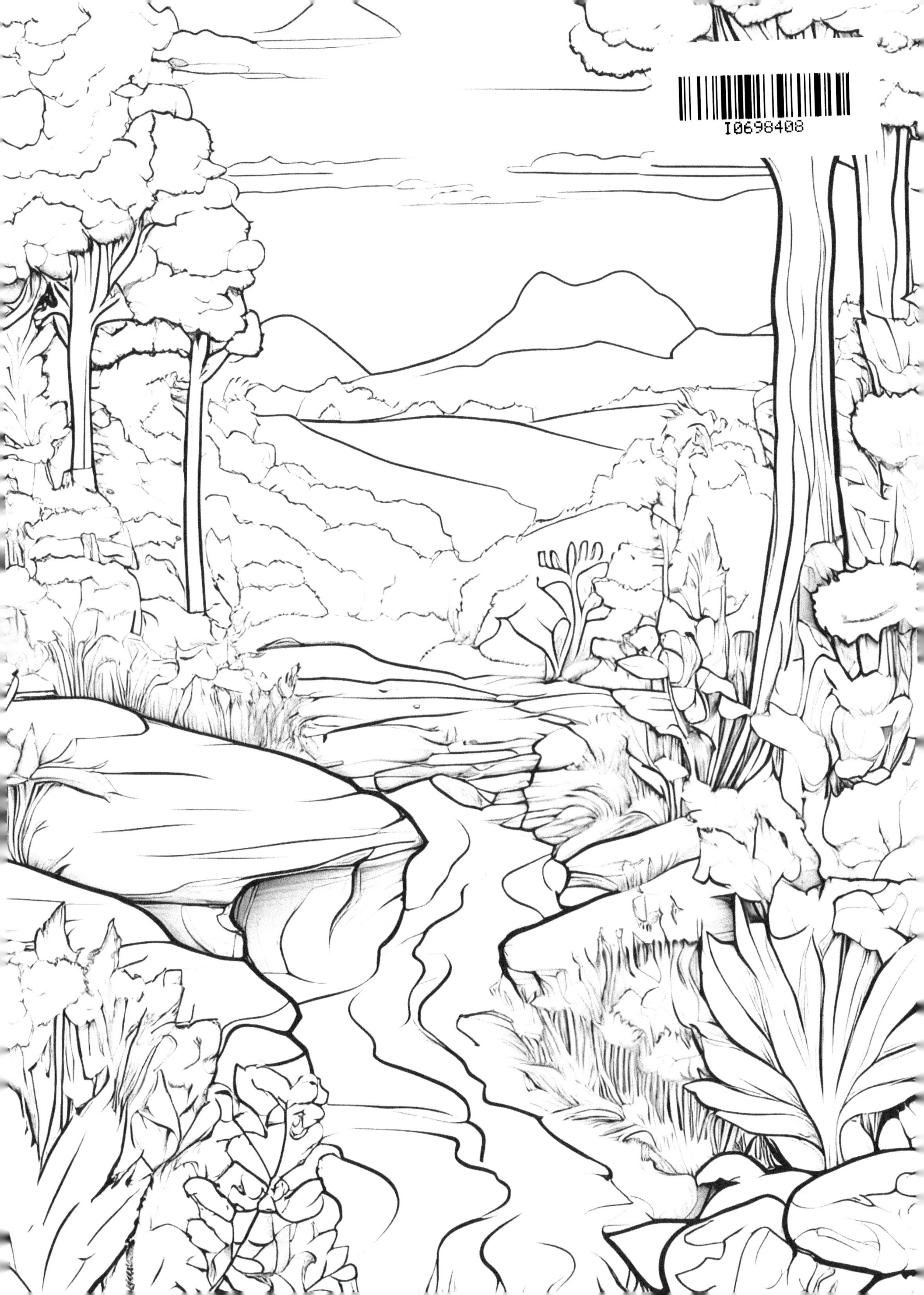
I0698408

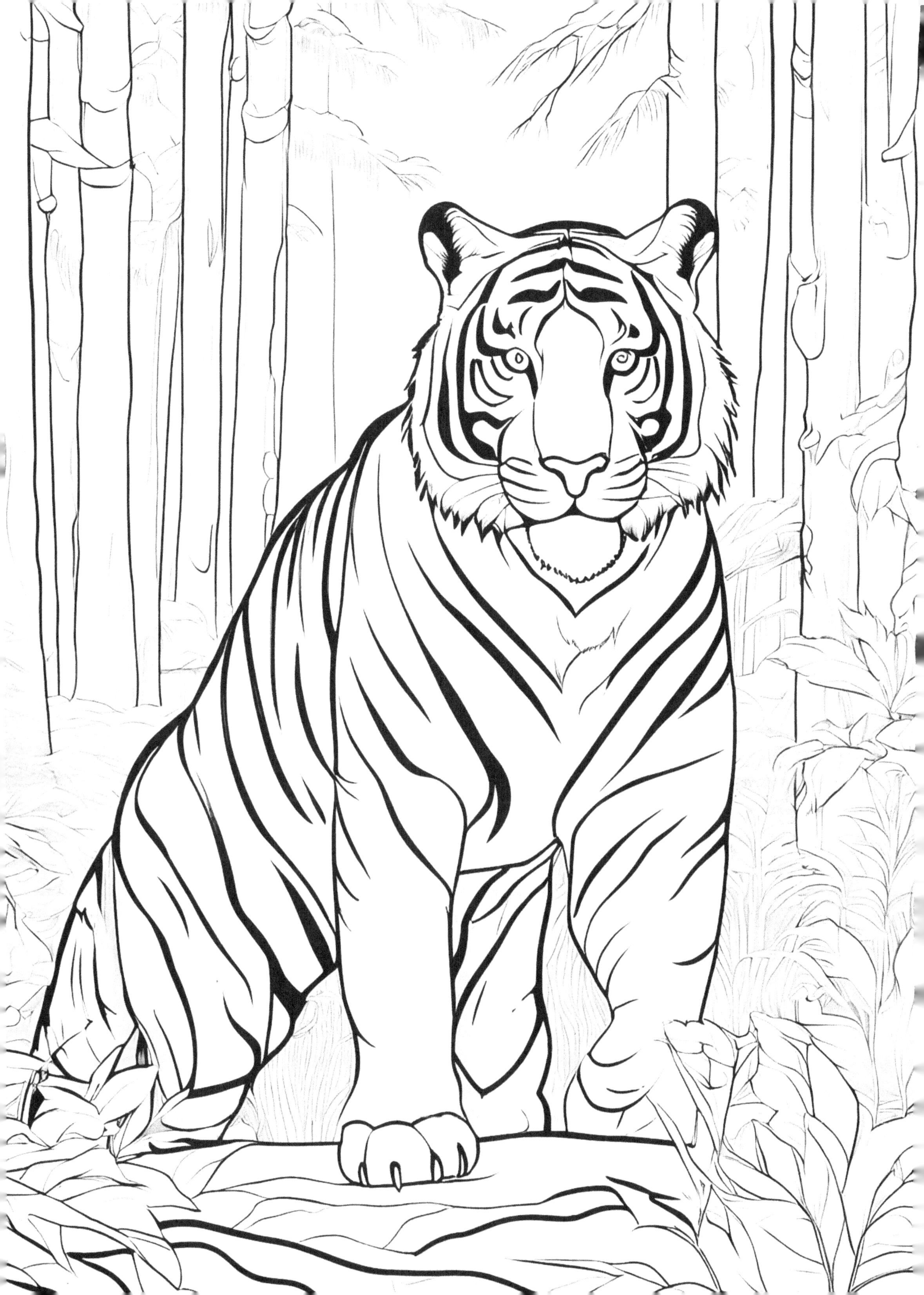

(PANTHERA TIGRIS ALTAICA) - FOUND MAINLY IN
RUSSIA, IT IS THE LARGEST OF THE TIGERS.

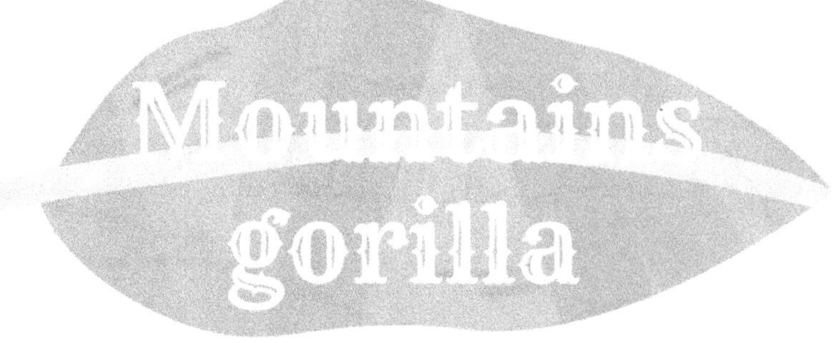

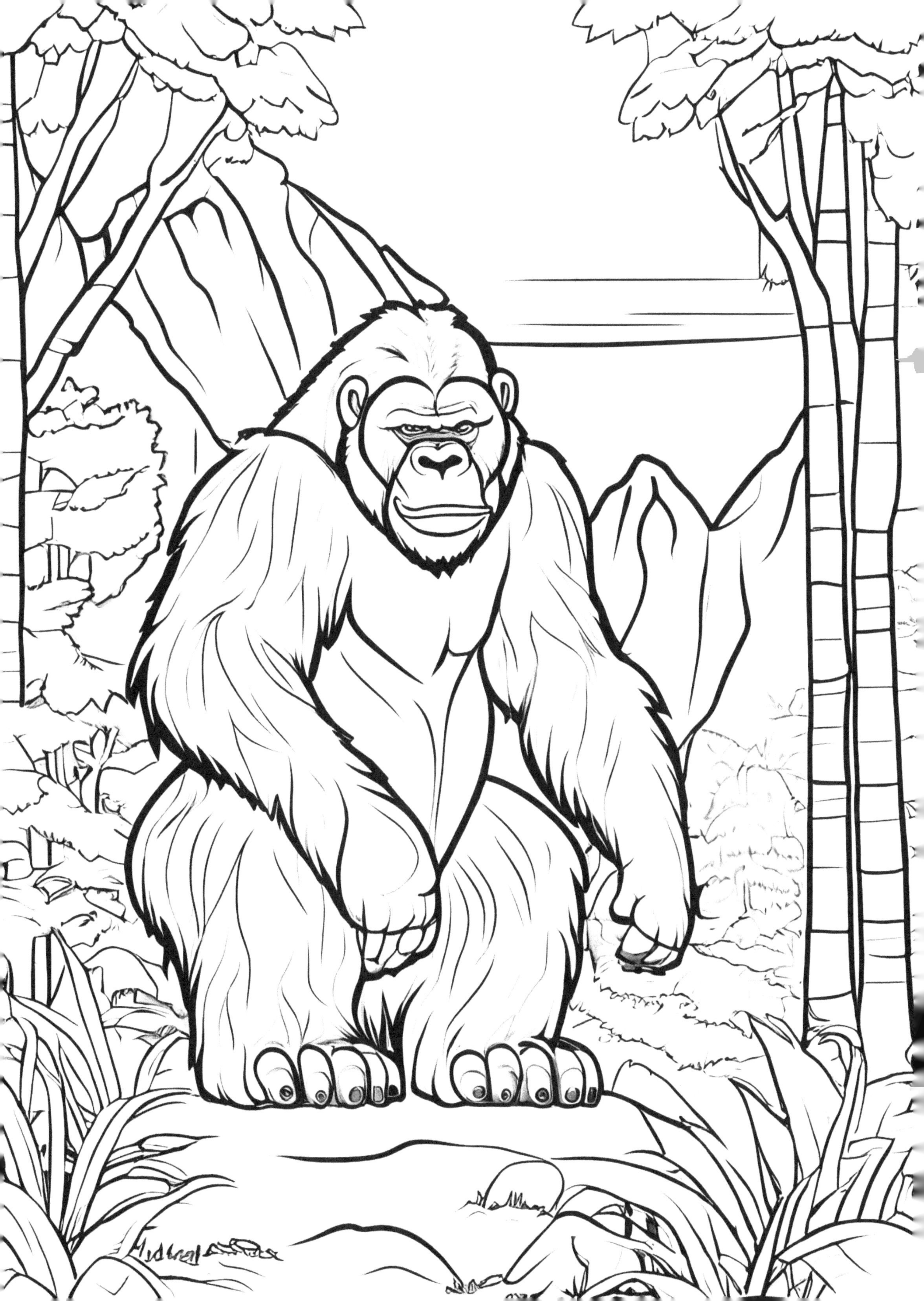

(GORILLA BERINGEI BERINGEI) – THEY LIVE IN THE
MOUNTAINOUS FORESTS OF CENTRAL AFRICA.

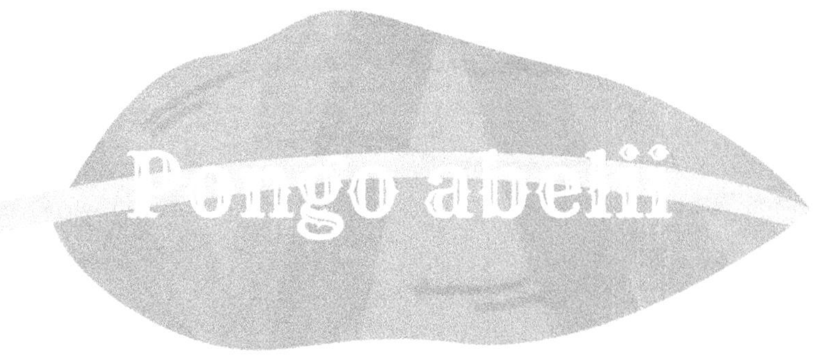

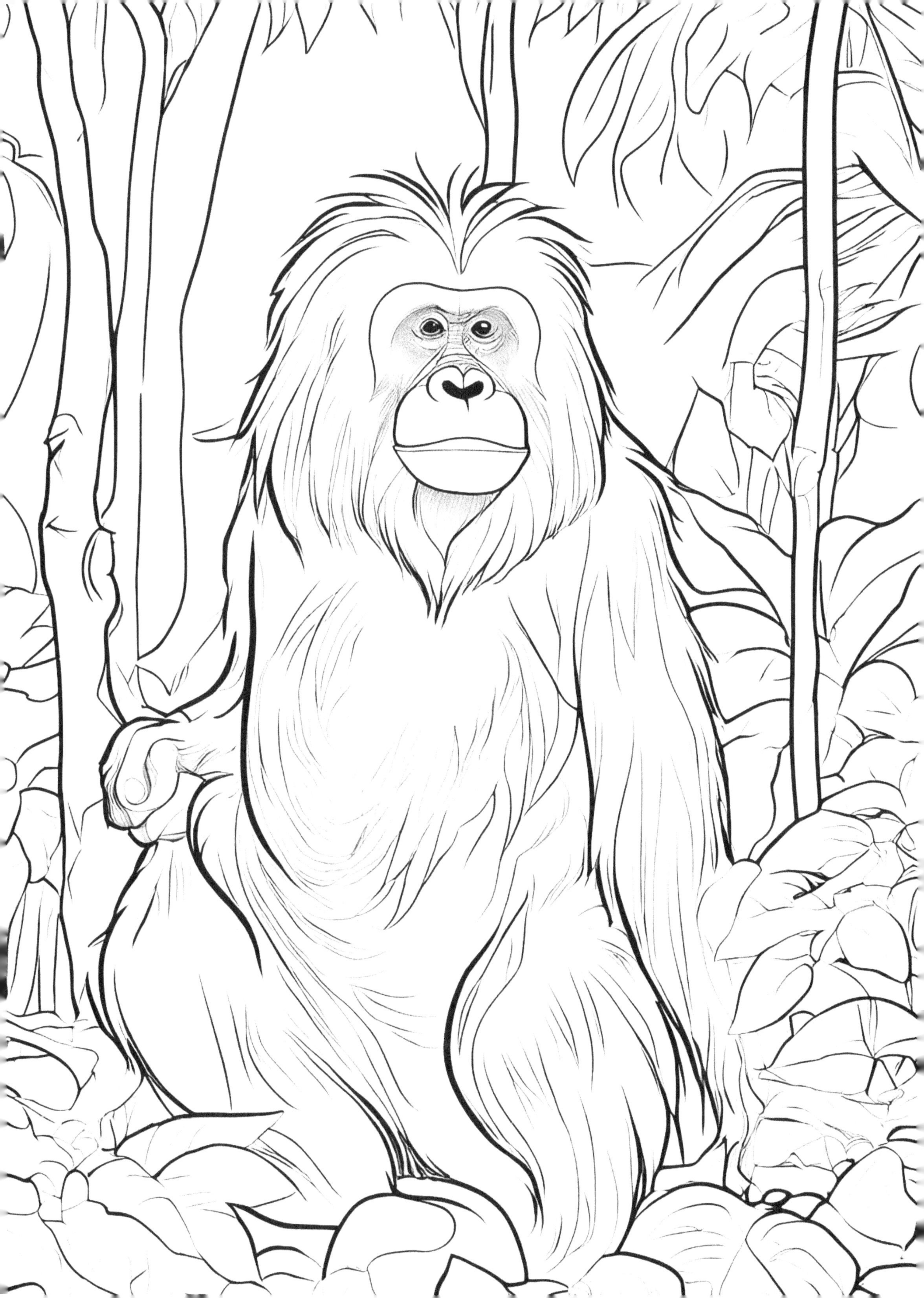

(PONGO ABELII) - SPECIES OF ORANGUTAN FOUND
ONLY ON THE ISLAND OF SUMATRA, INDONESIA.

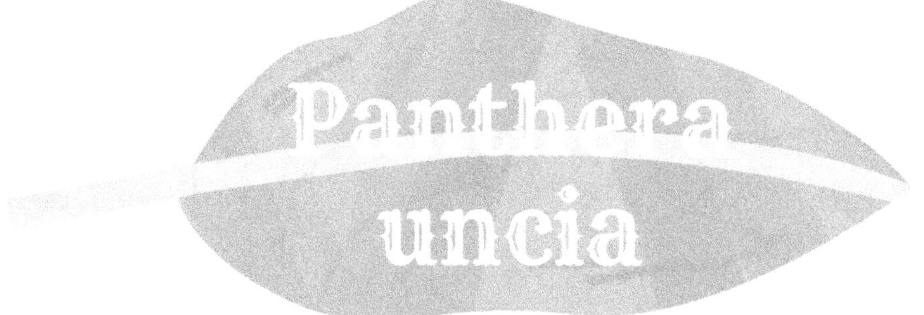

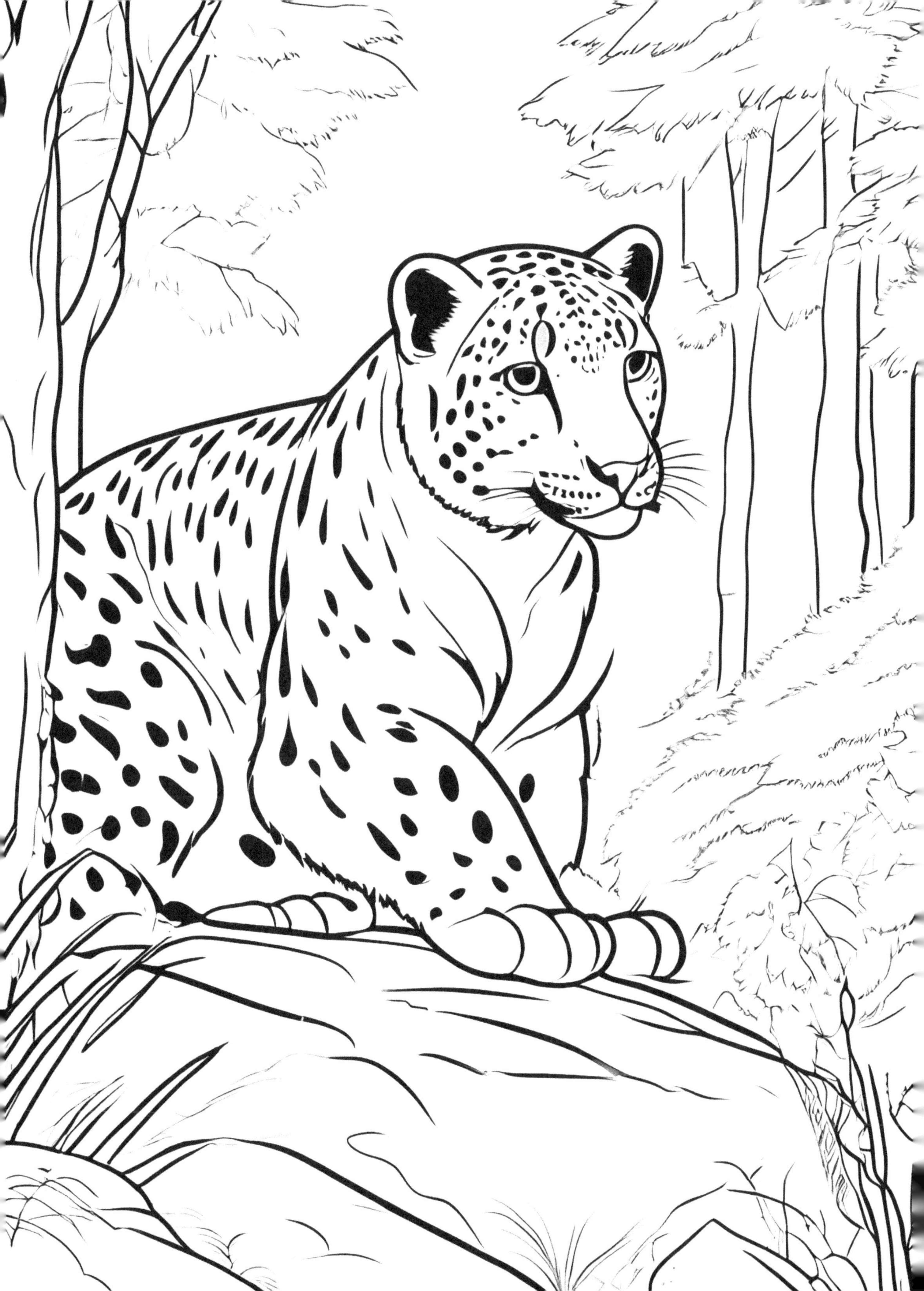

(PANTHERA UNCIA) - NATIVE TO THE
MOUNTAINS OF CENTRAL ASIA.

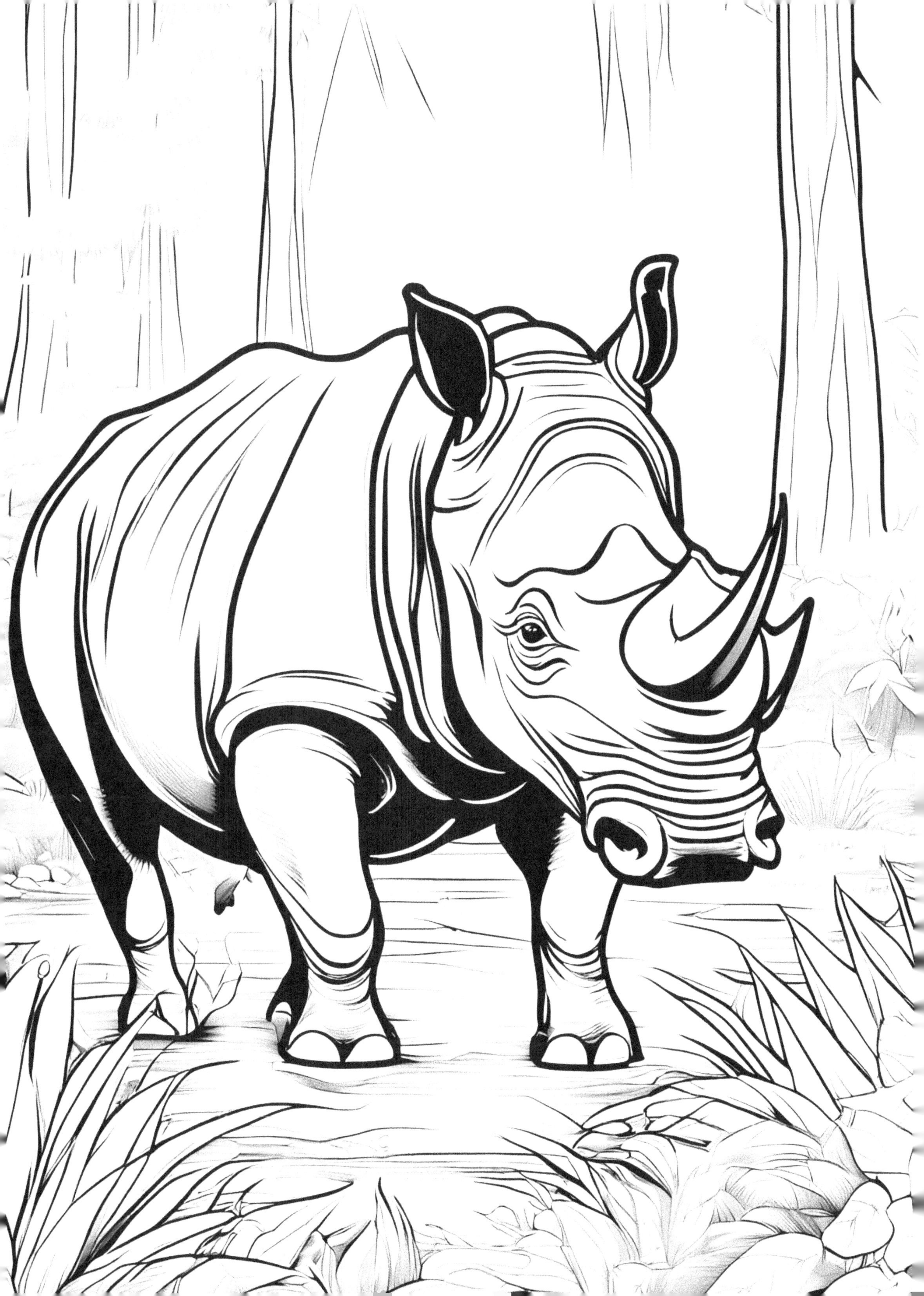

(RHINOCEROS SONDAICUS) - ONE OF THE MOST ENDANGERED
RHINO SPECIES, FOUND MAINLY IN INDONESIA.

Pangolin

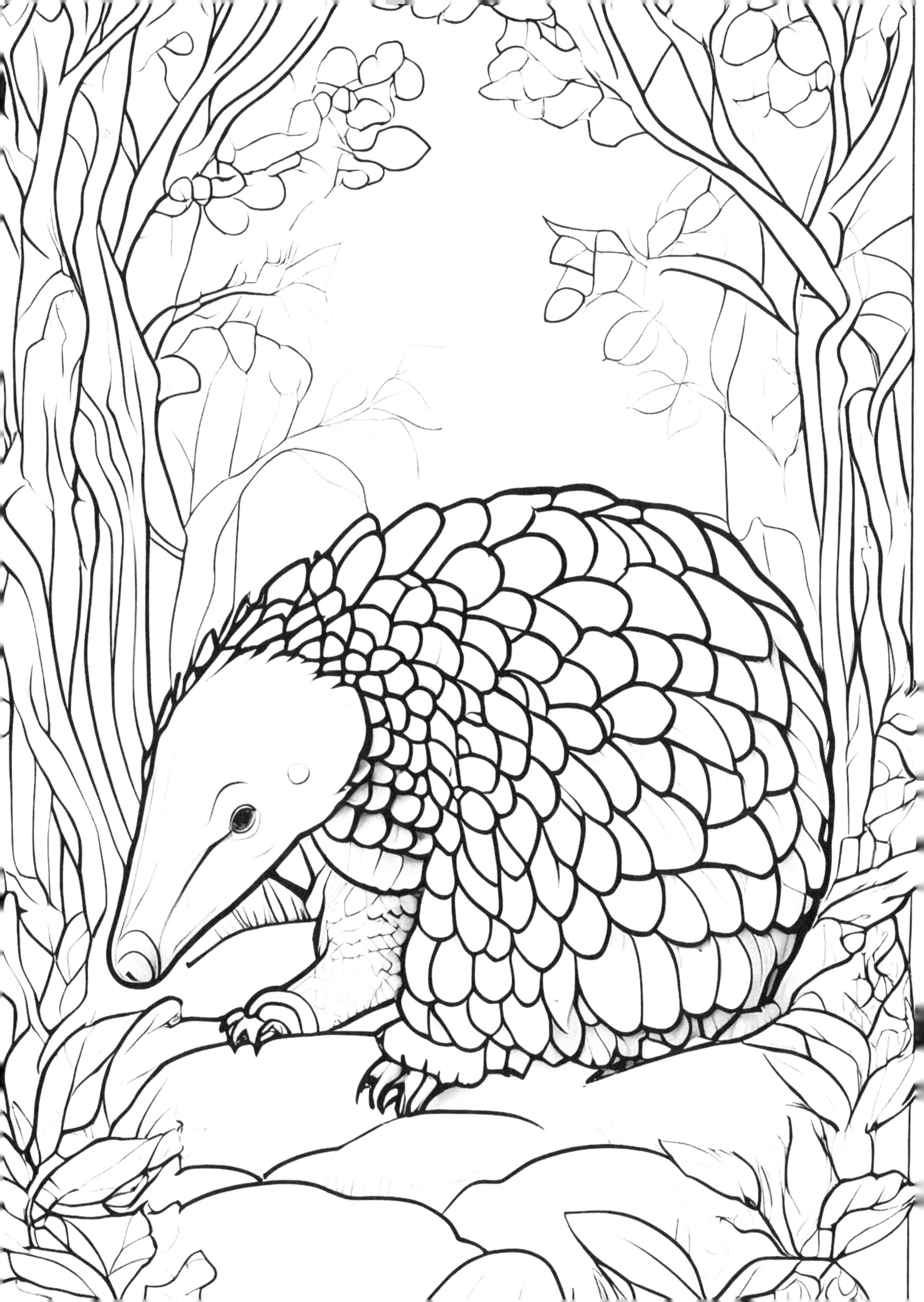

(PANGOLIN) - SEVERAL SPECIES OF THESE MAMMALS ARE
CRITICALLY ENDANGERED DUE TO ILLEGAL HUNTING.

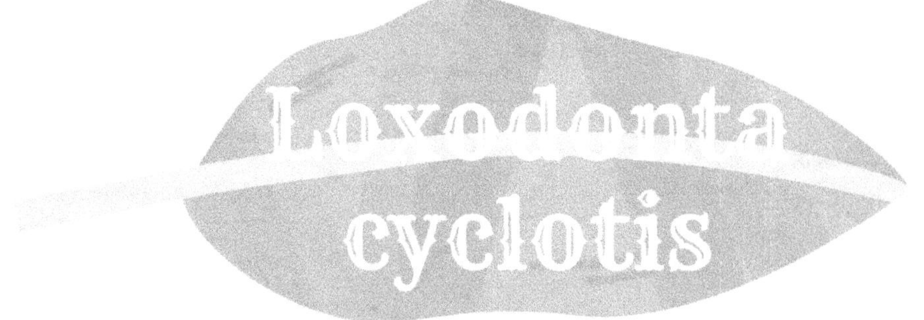

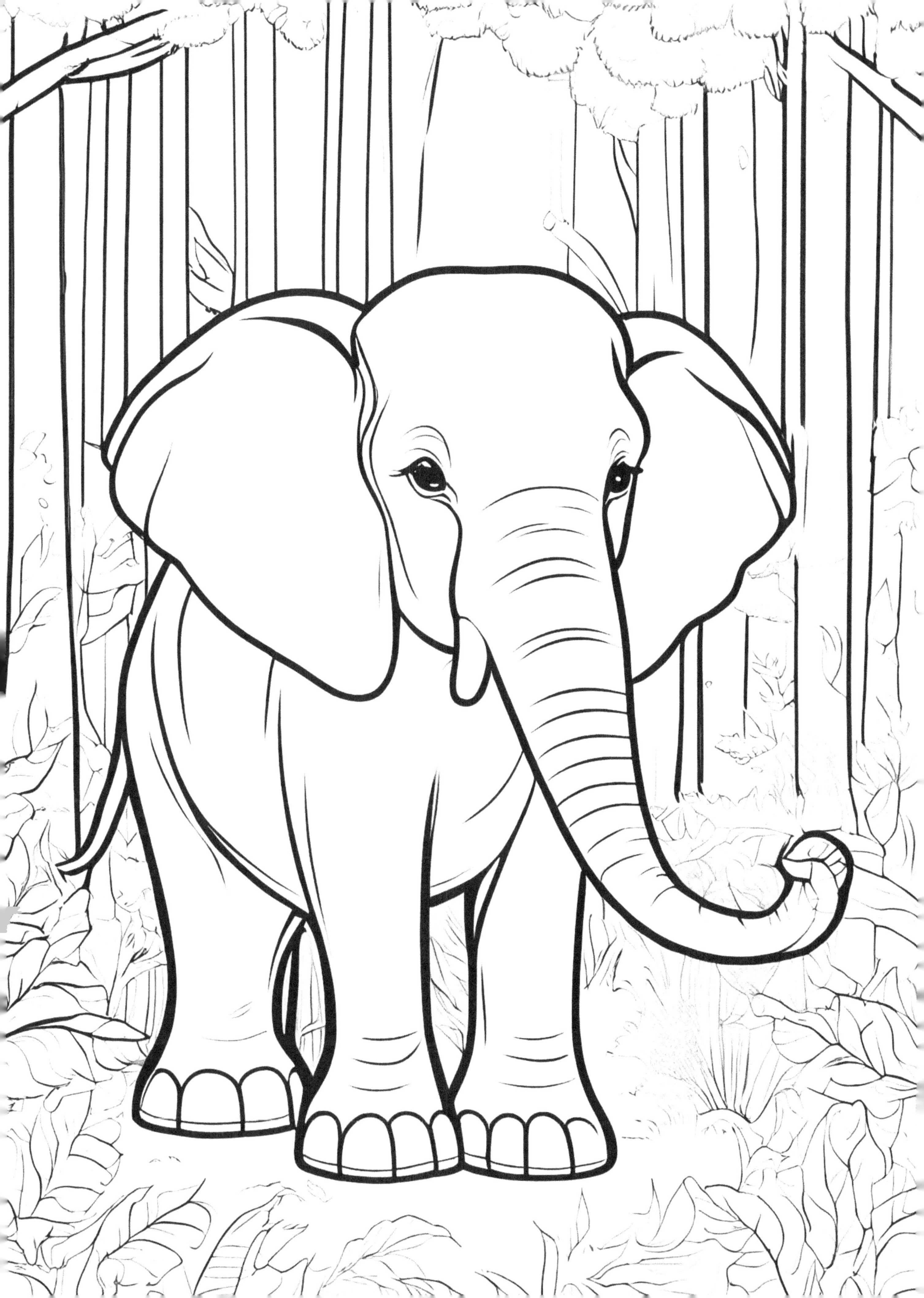

(LOXODONTA CYCLOTIS) - SMALLER THAN ITS SAVANNAH
COUSIN, IT INHABITS DENSE FORESTS IN AFRICA.

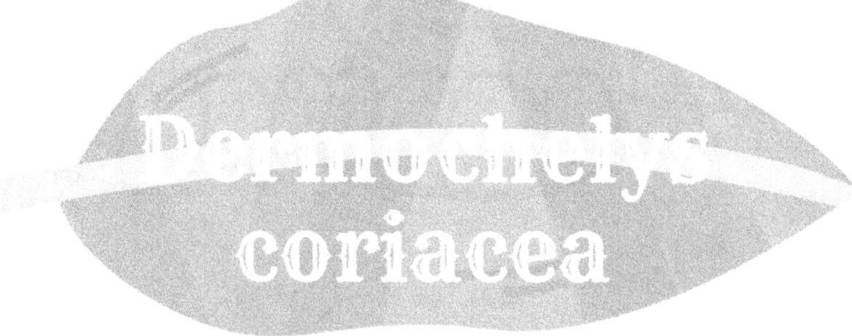

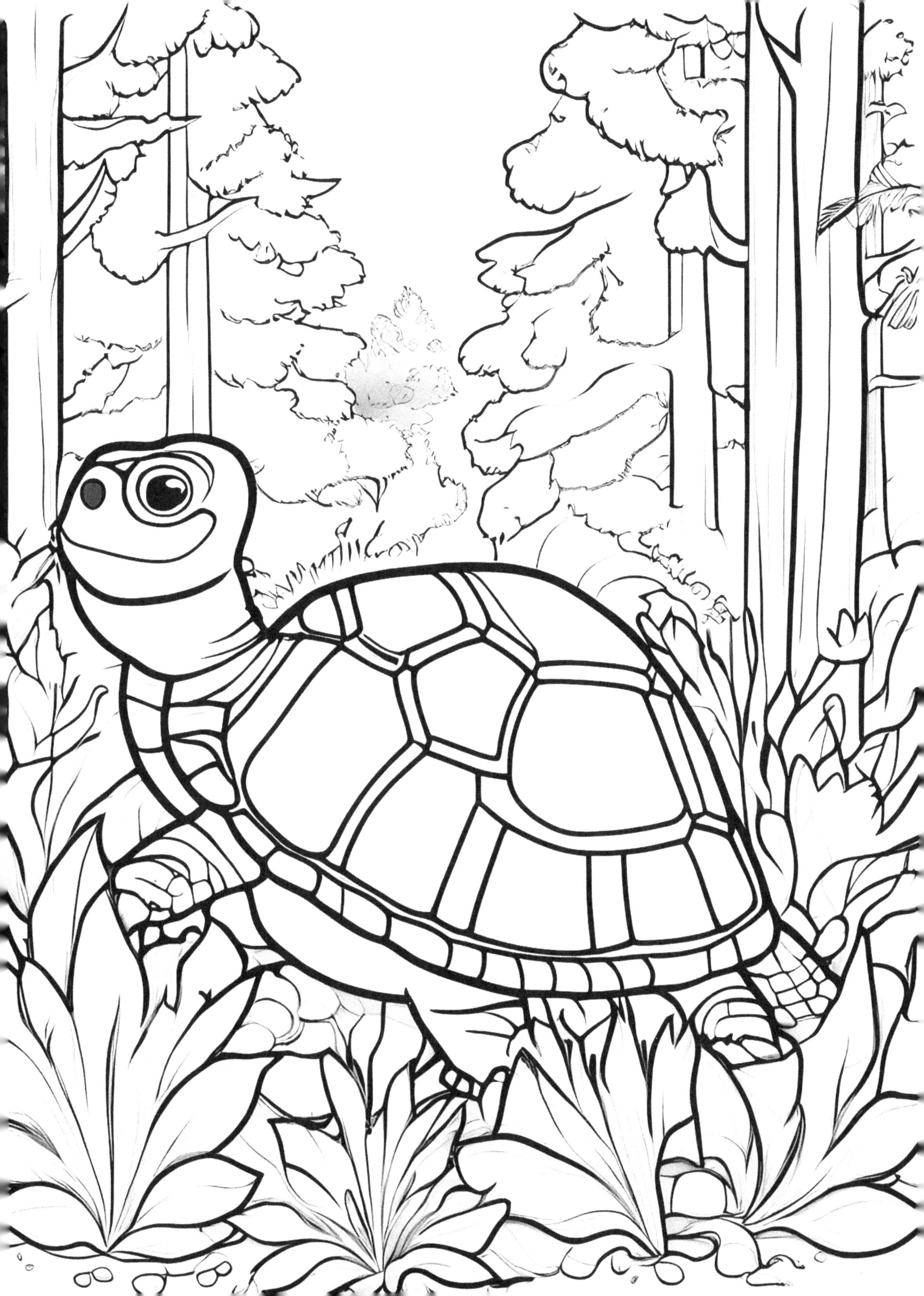

(DERMOCHELYS CORIACEA) - THE LARGEST
OF ALL TURTLE SPECIES.

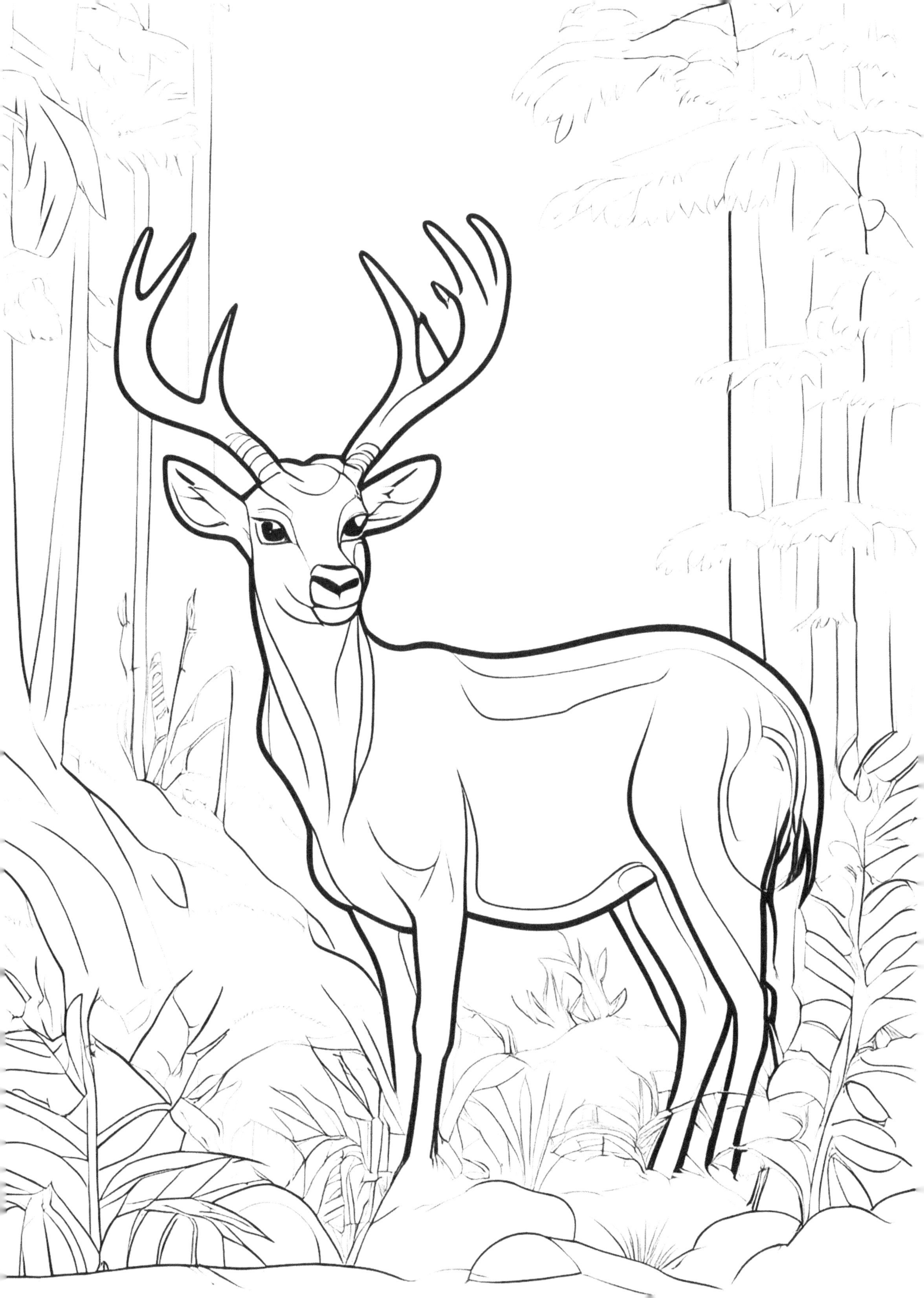

(PSEUDORYX NGHETINHENSIS) - ALSO KNOWN AS THE "UNICORN OF ASIA", IT IS EXTREMELY RARE IN VIETNAM AND LAOS.

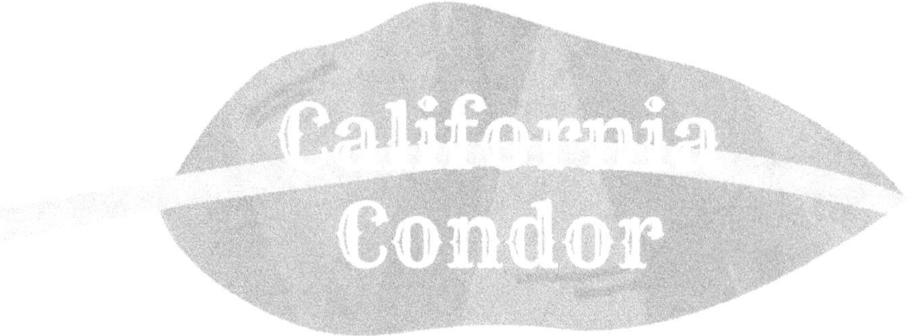

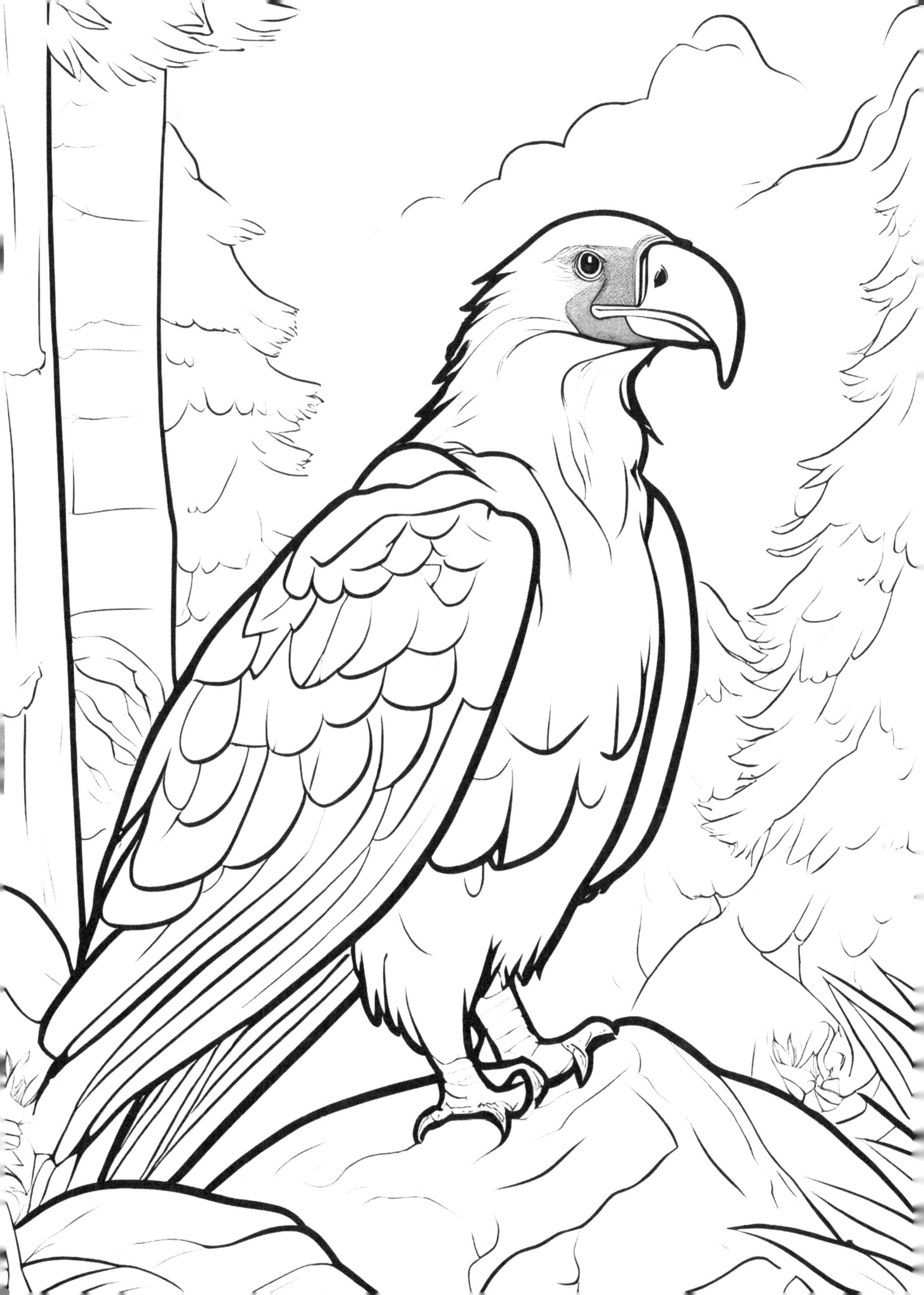

(GYMNOGYPS CALIFORNIANUS) - A
LARGE AMERICAN VULTURE.

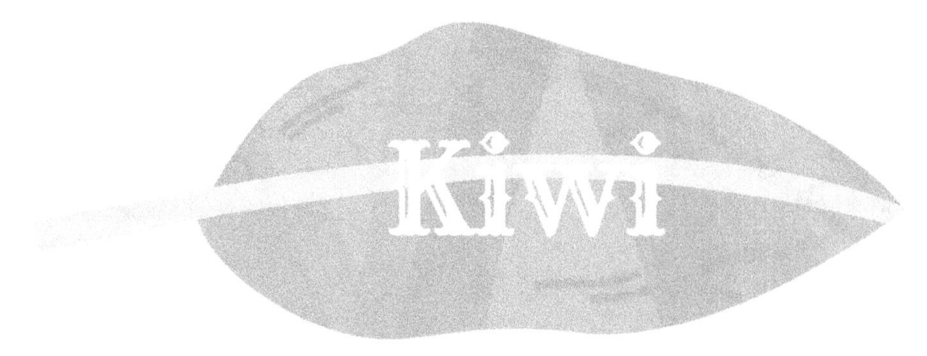

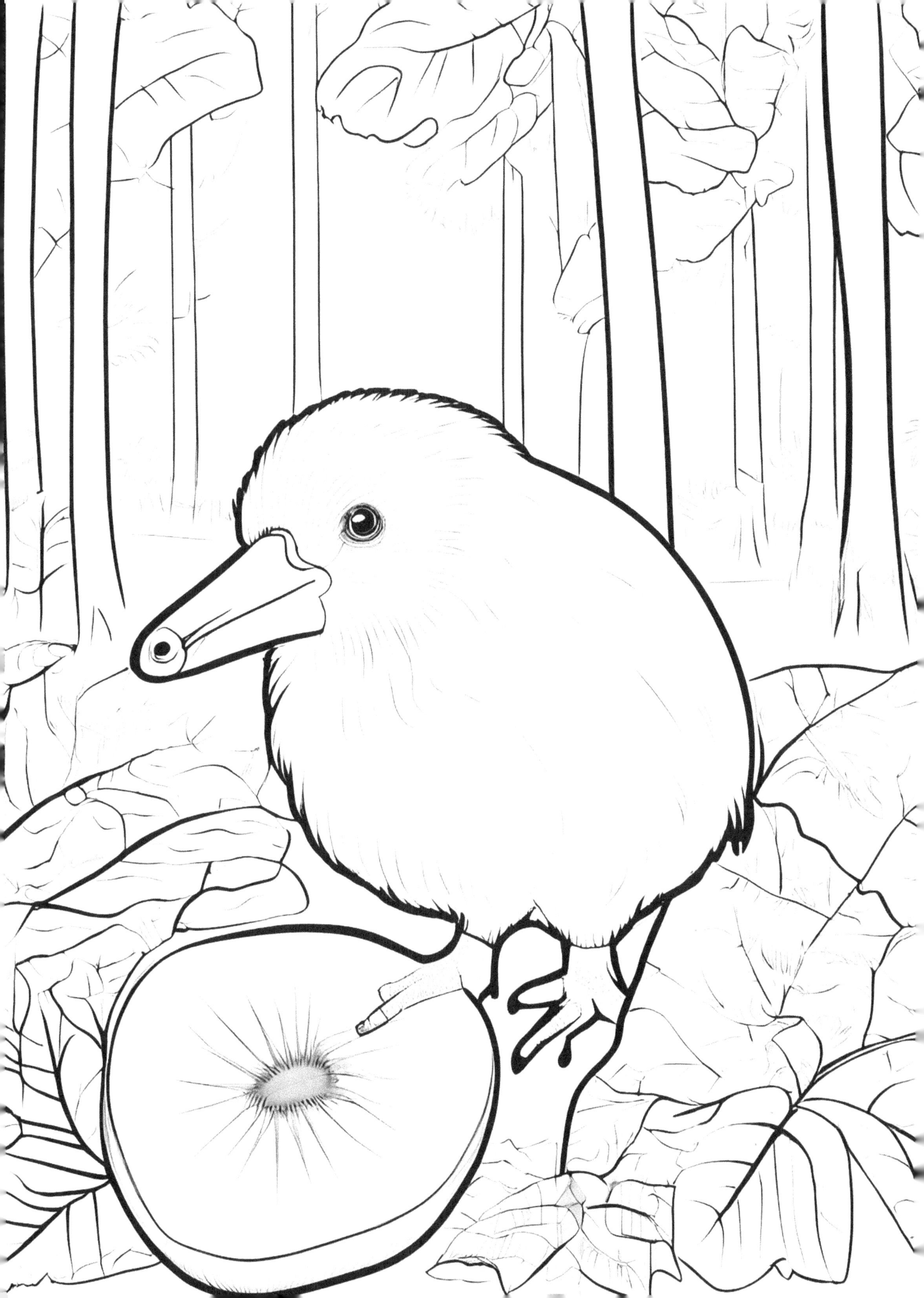

(KIWI) – SEVERAL SPECIES OF THIS FLIGHTLESS
BIRD FROM NEW ZEALAND ARE AT RISK.

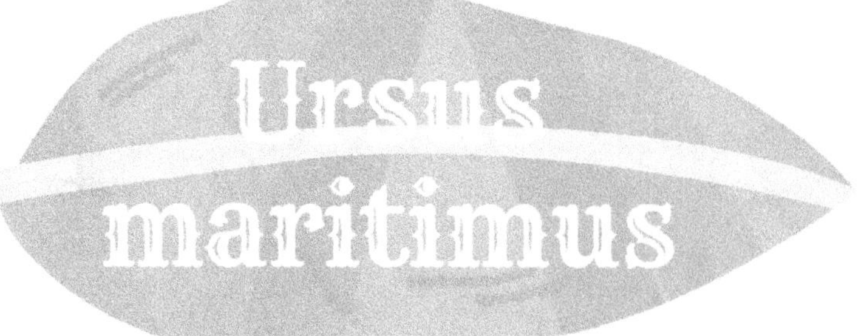

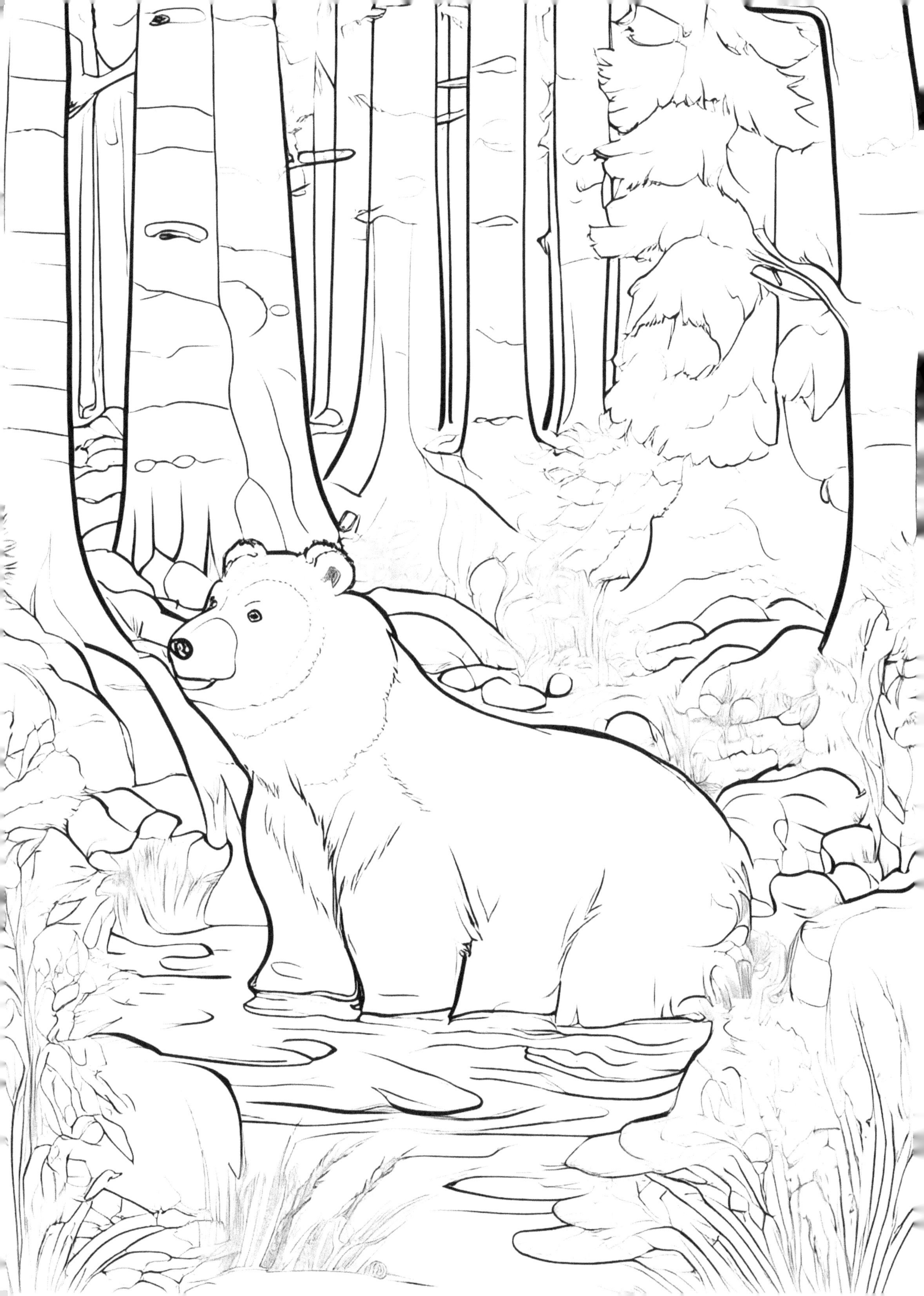

(URSUS MARITIMUS) - VULNERABLE DUE TO LOSS OF ITS SEA
ICE HABITAT.

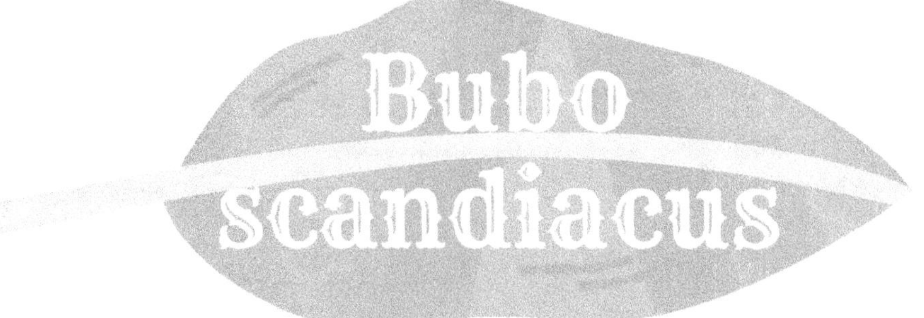

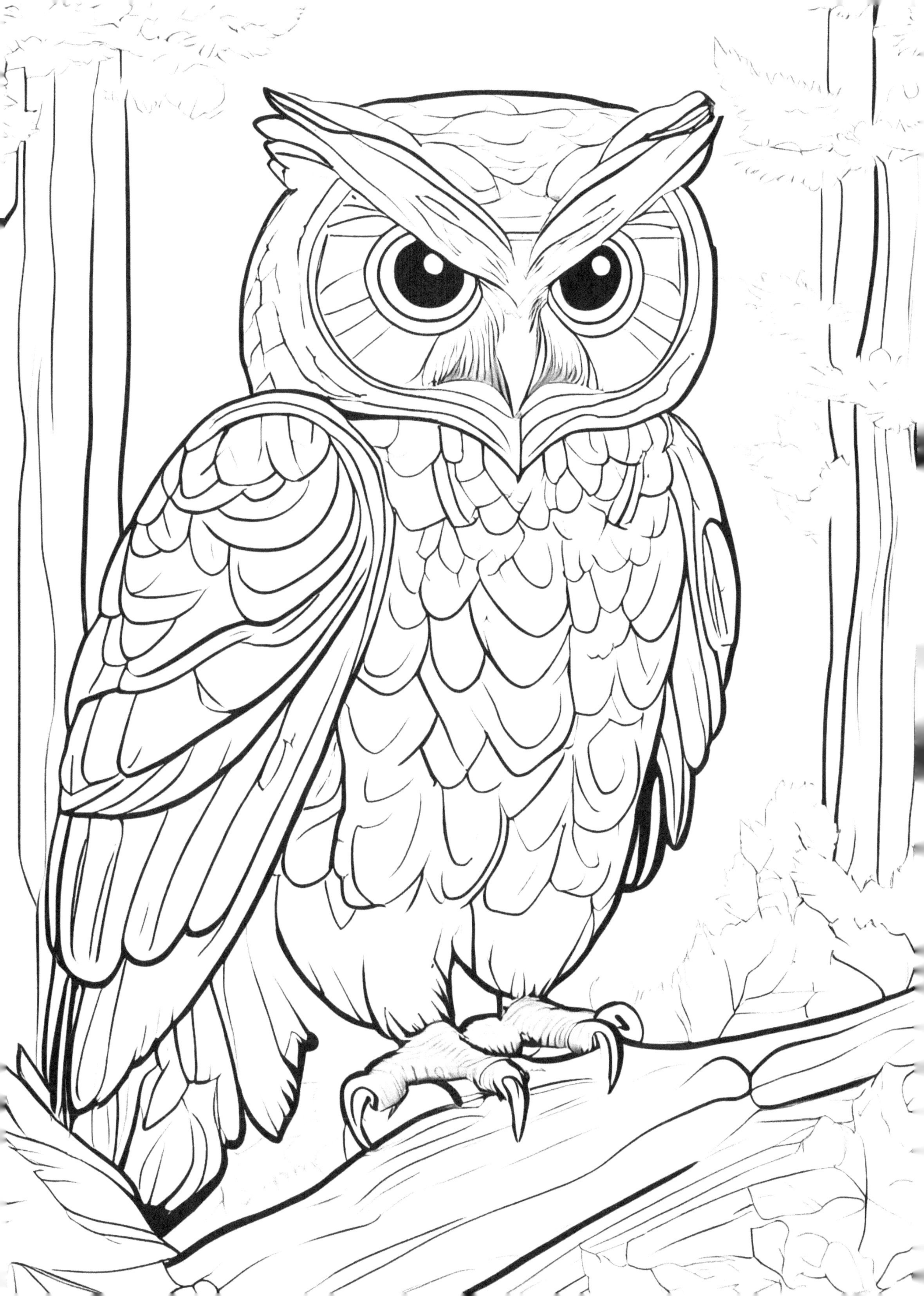

(BUBO SCANDIACUS) - DEPENDENT ON COLD ARCTIC
HABITATS.

Panthera
tigris
jacksoni

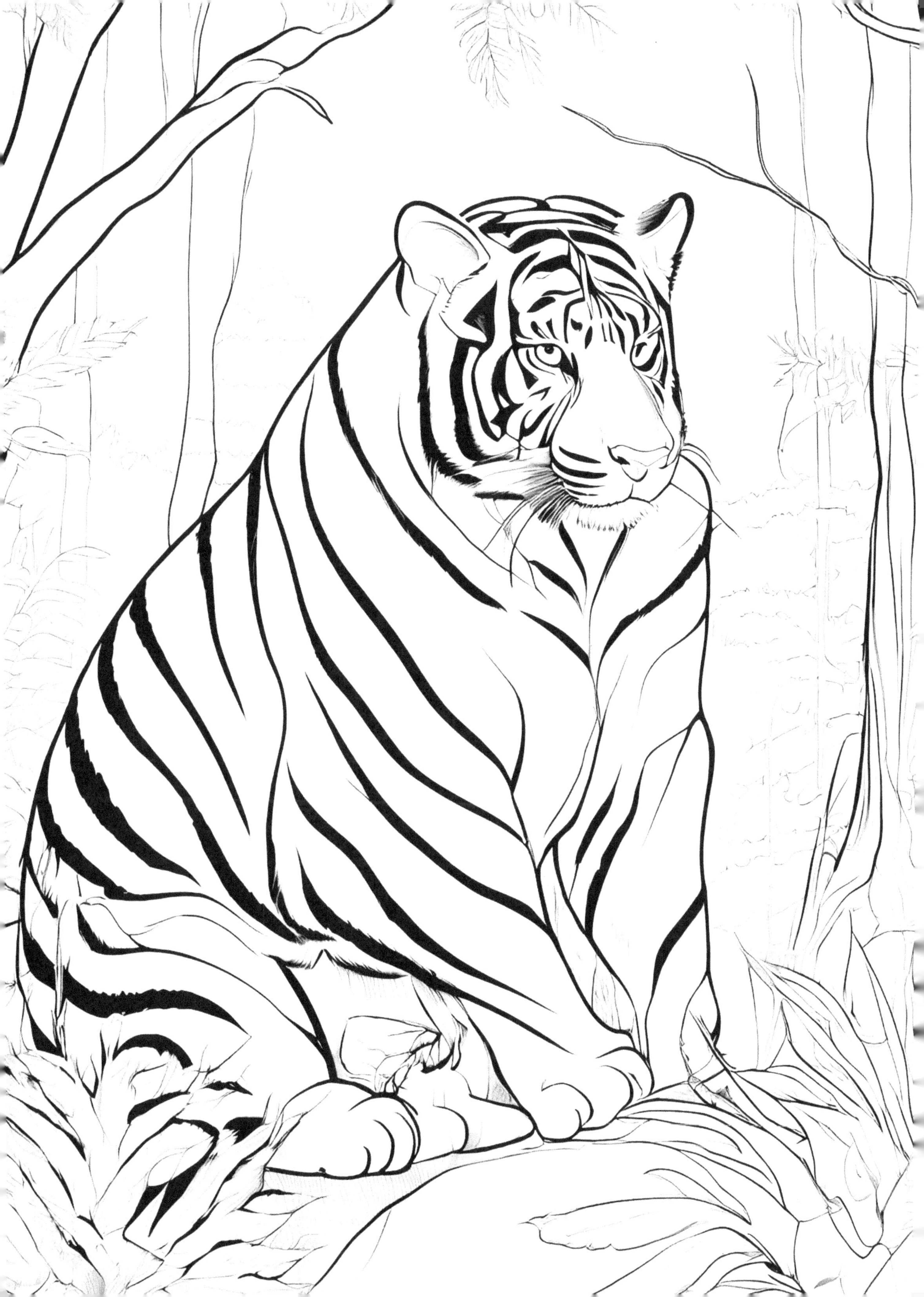

(PANTHERA TIGRIS JACKSONI) - A SUBSPECIES OF
TIGER FOUND ON THE MALAY PENINSULA.

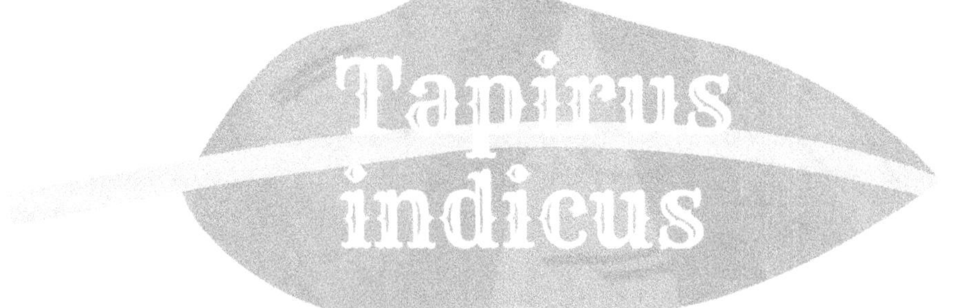

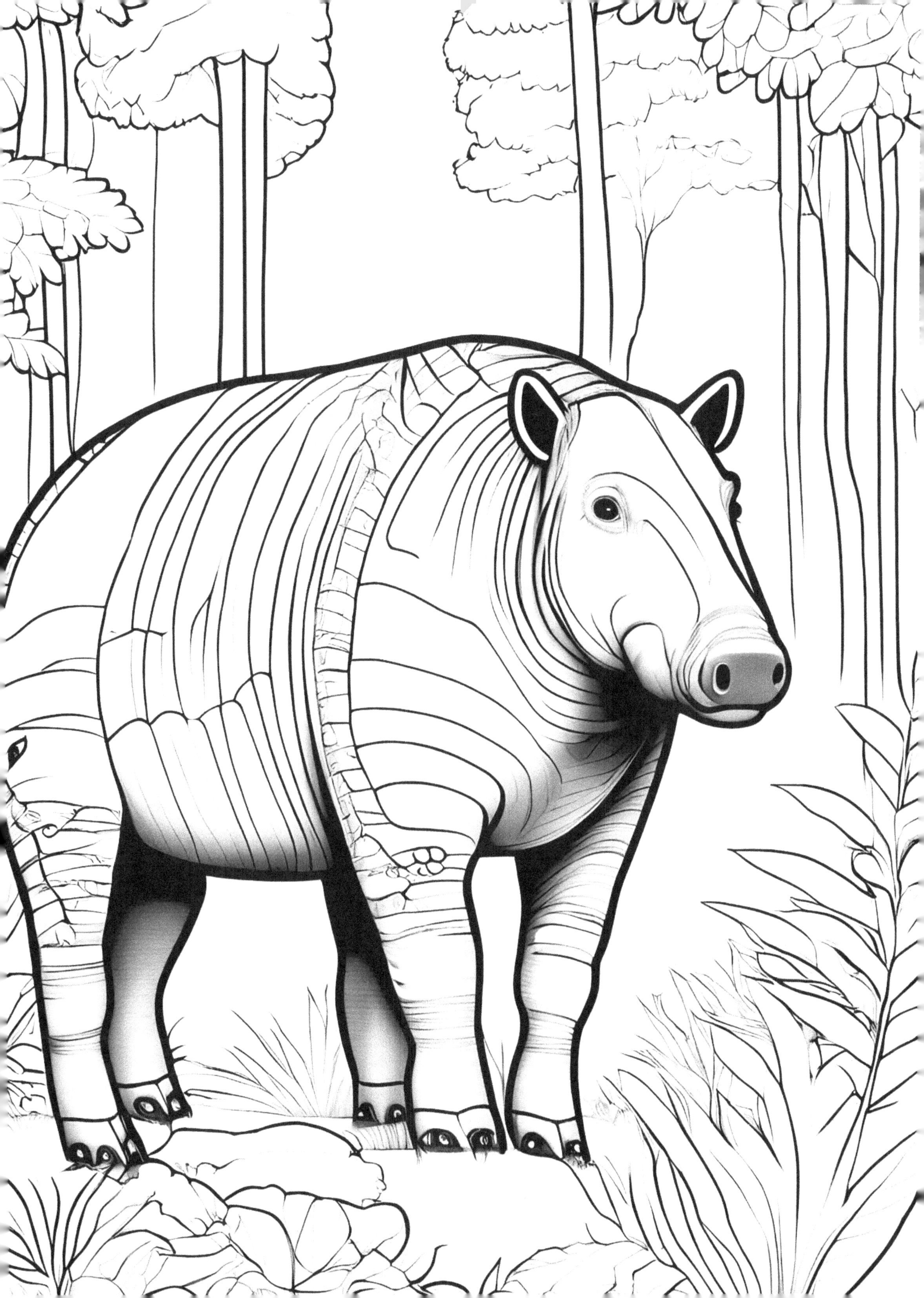

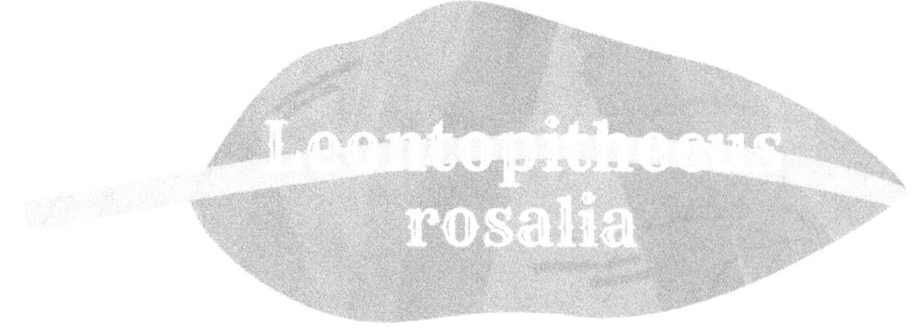
Leontopithecus
rosalia

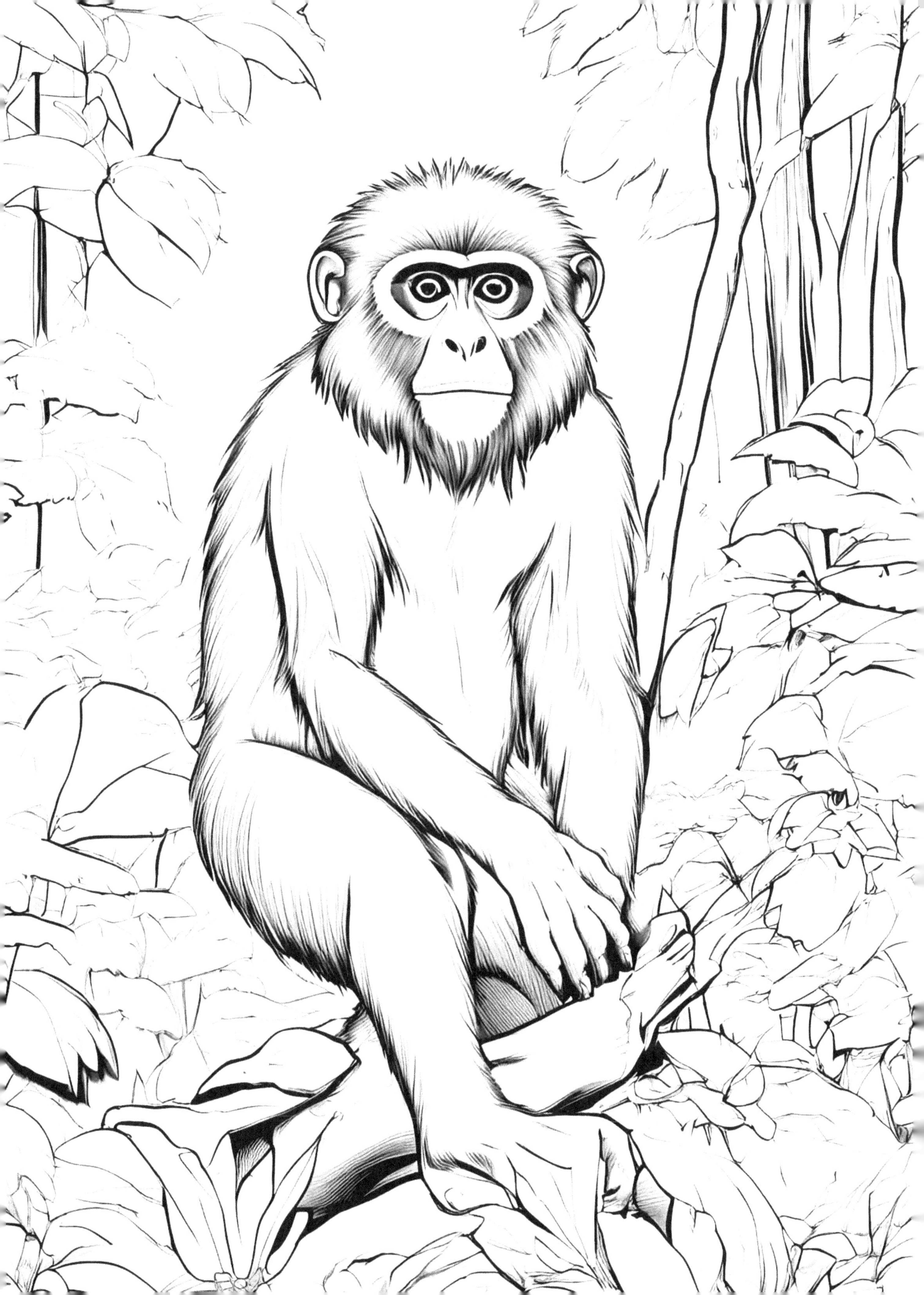

(LEONTOPITHECUS ROSALIA) – ENDEMIC TO BRAZILIAN FORESTS.

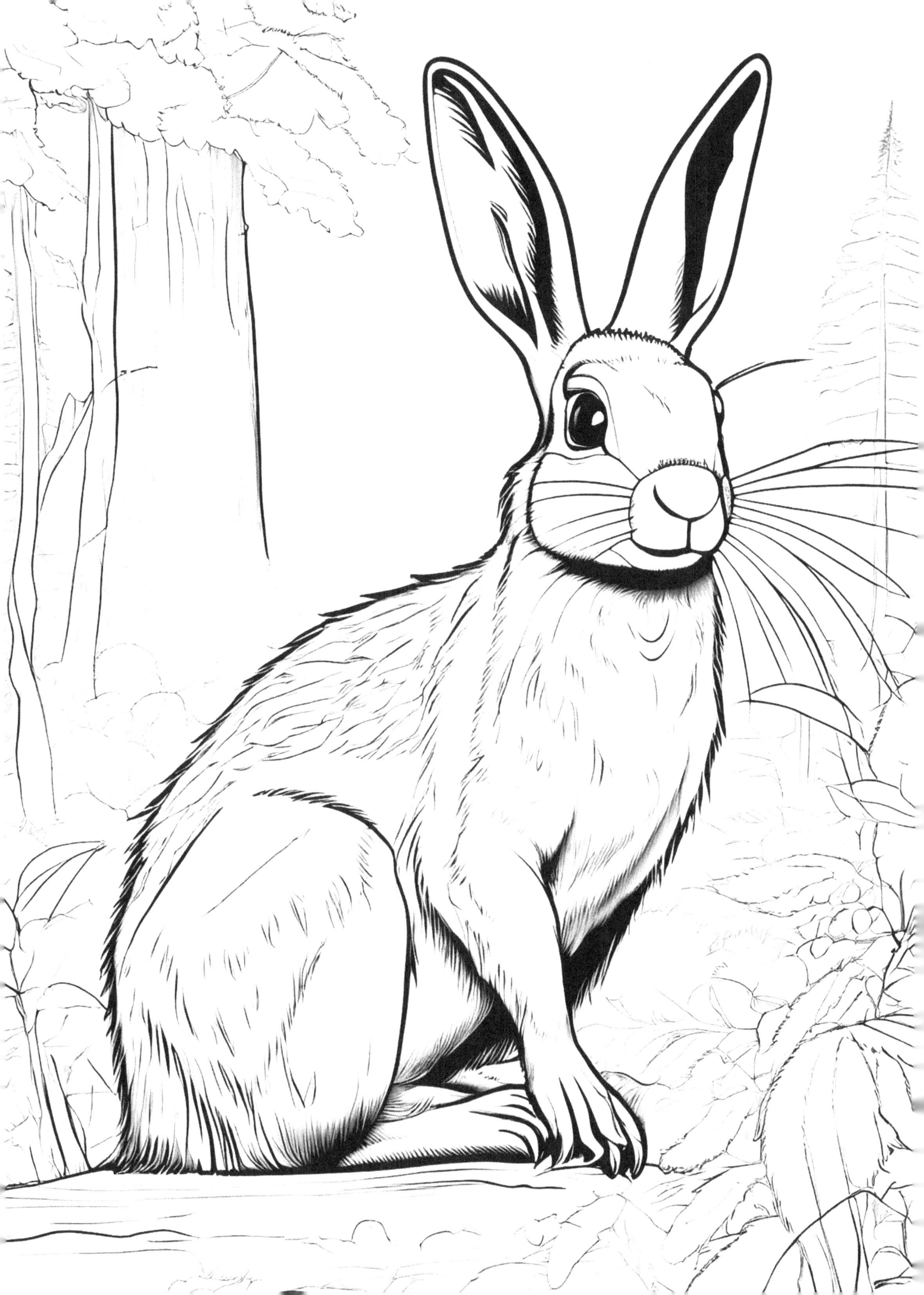

(SYLVILAGUS BACHMANI RIPARIUS) - ONE OF THE MOST ENDANGERED MAMMAL SPECIES IN
NORTH AMERICA.

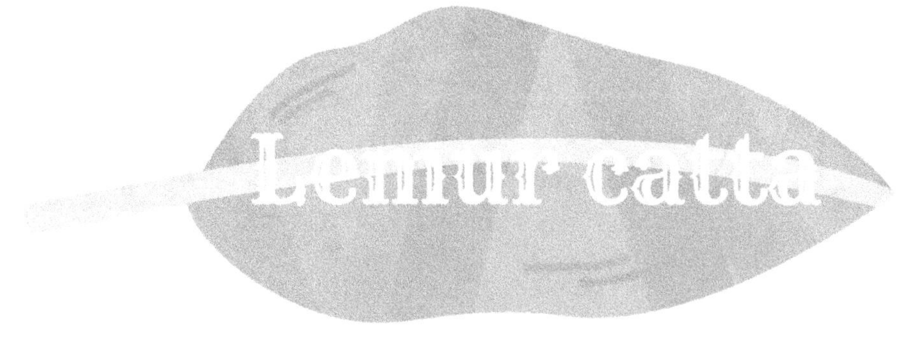
Lemur catta

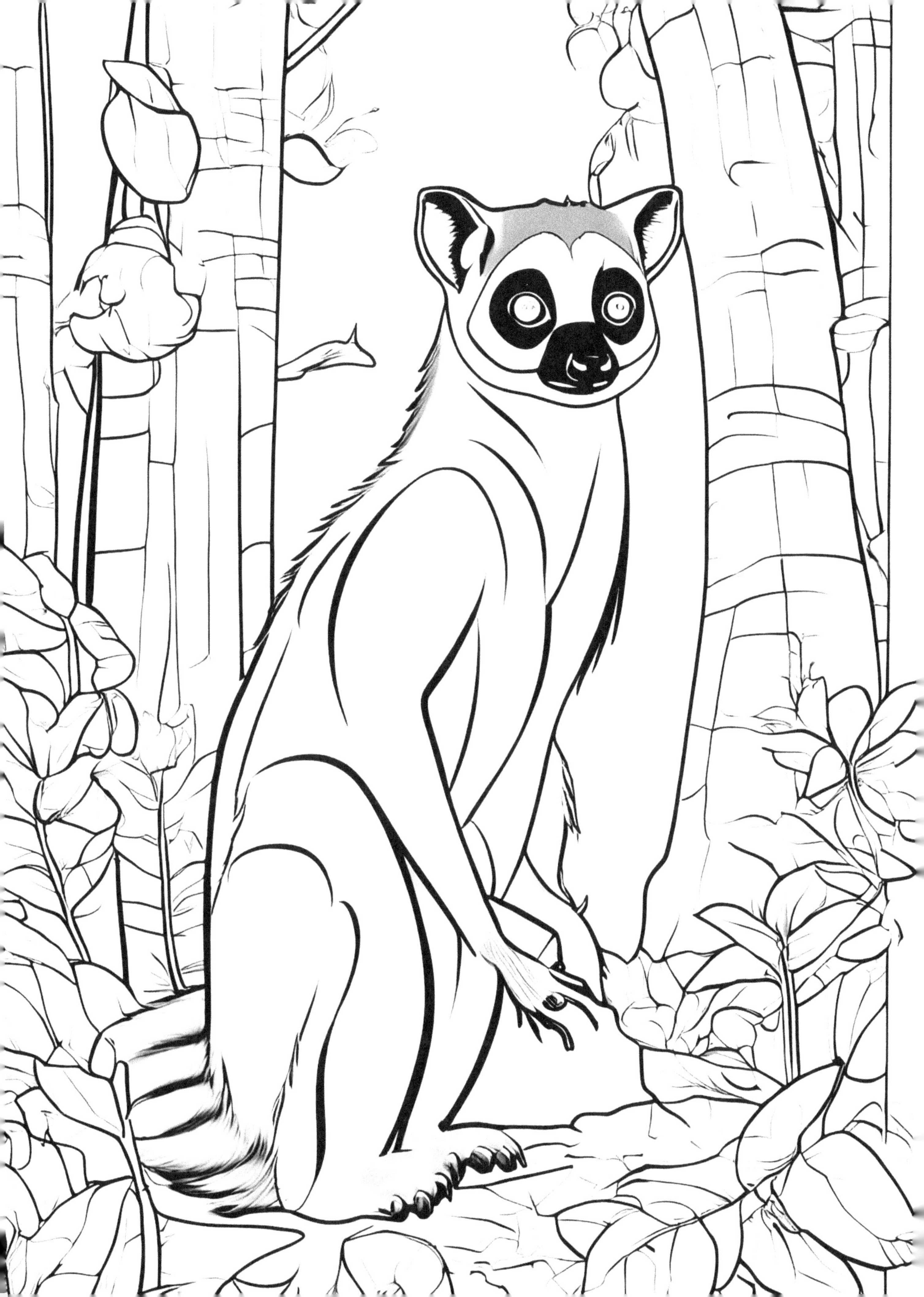

(LEMUR CATTA) - ENDEMIC TO MADAGASCAR.

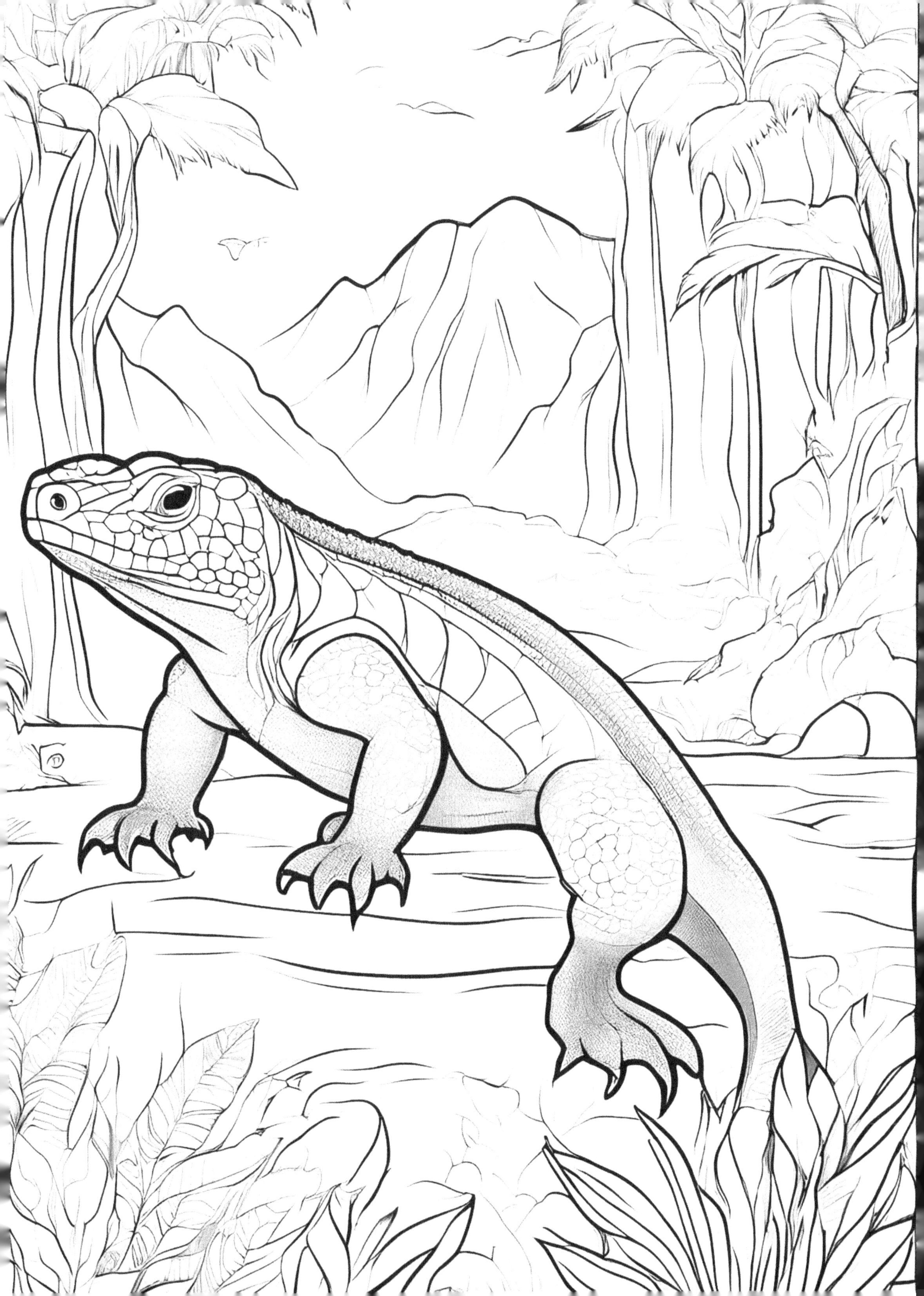

(VARANUS KOMODOENSIS) — THE LARGEST LIZARD IN THE WORLD,
FOUND IN INDONESIA.

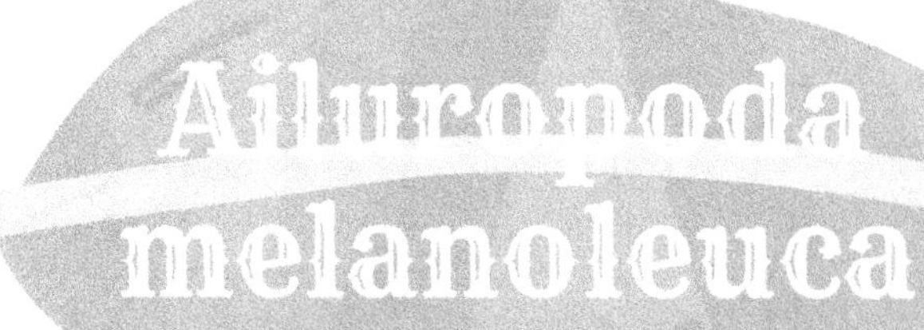

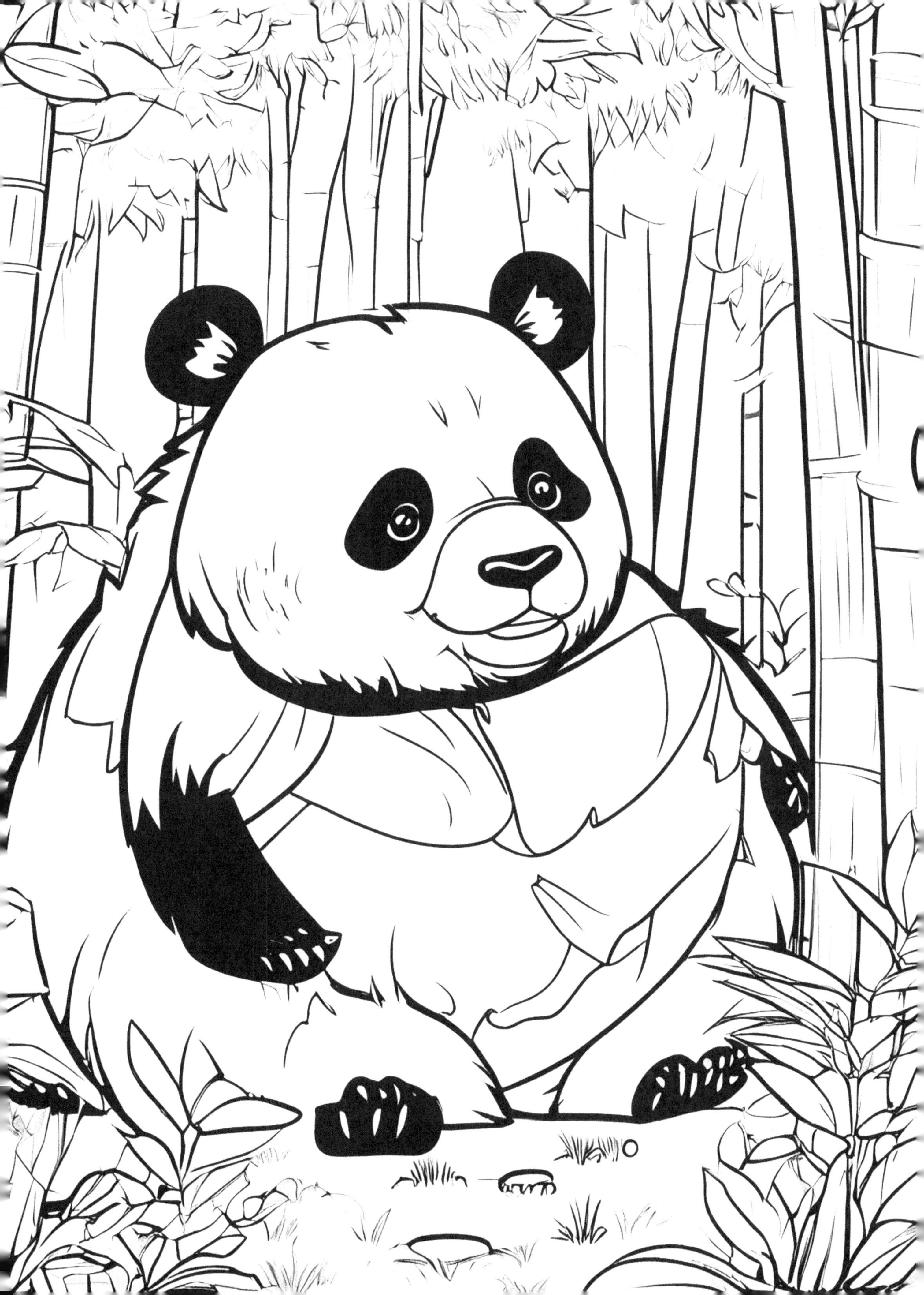

(AILUROPODA MELANOLEUCA) - AN ICON OF CONSERVATION,
NATIVE TO CHINA.

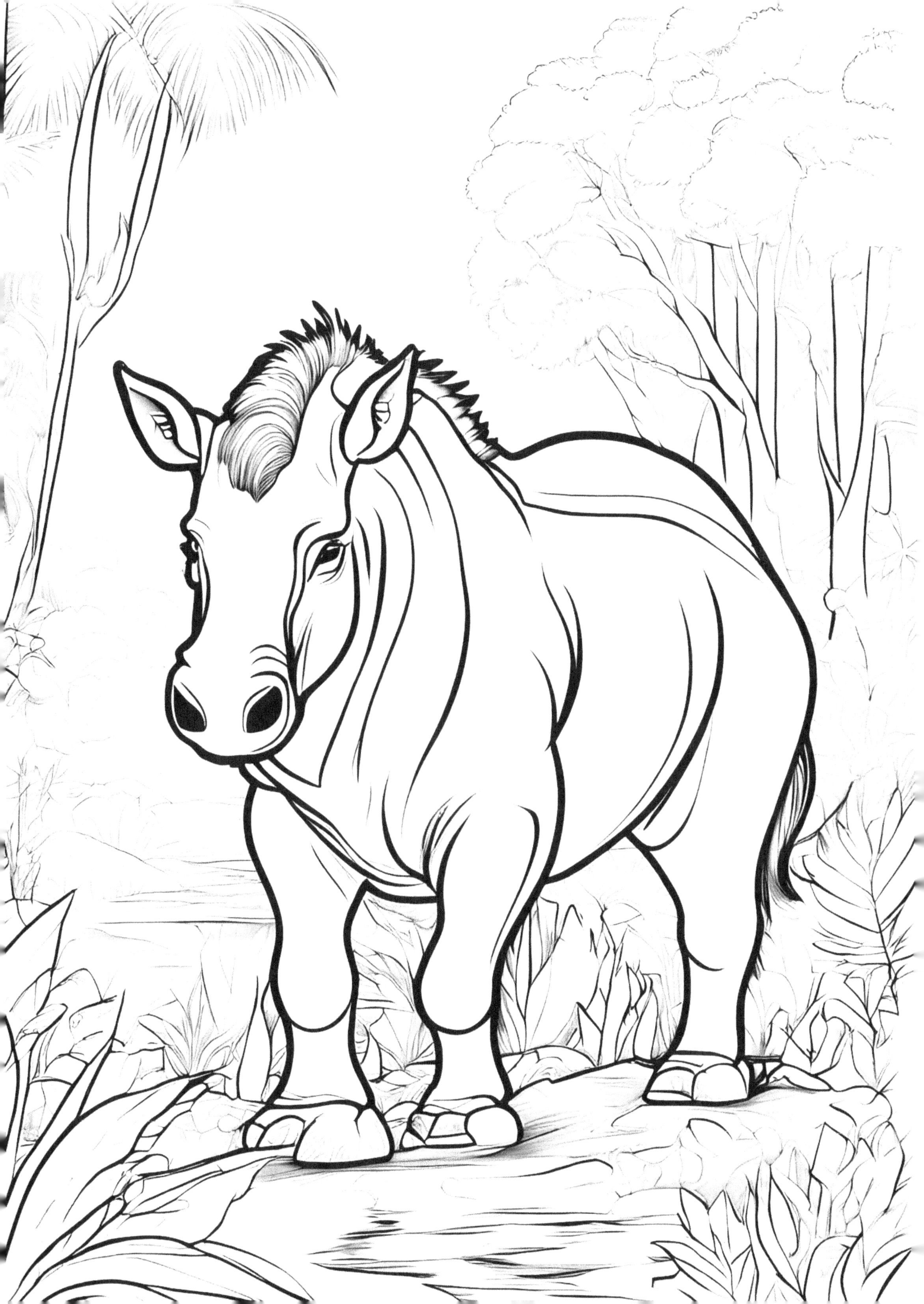

(DICERORHINUS SUMATRENSIS) - ONE OF THE SMALLEST
SPECIES OF RHINOS.

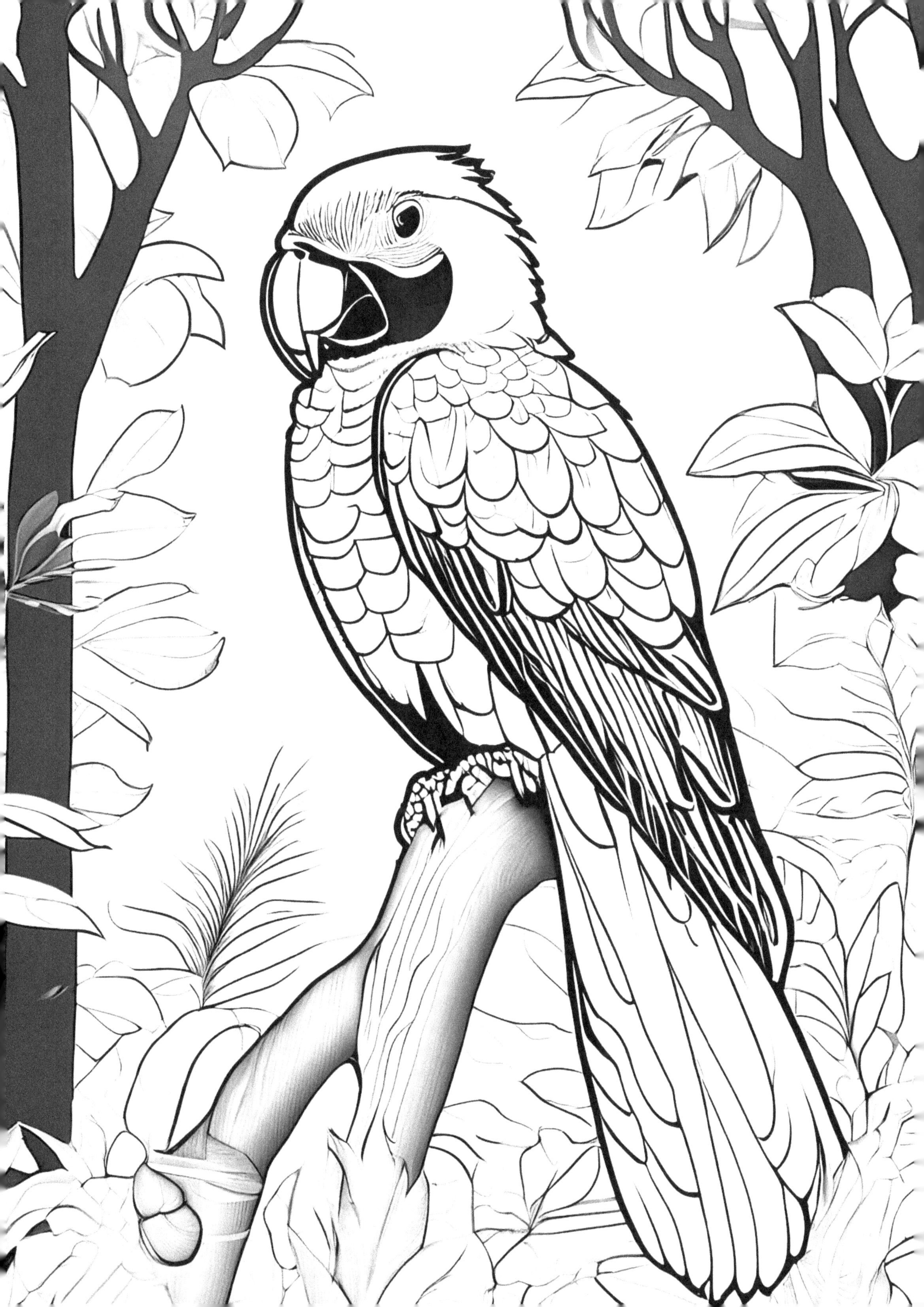

(ANODORHYNCHUS HYACINTHINUS) - THE LARGEST OF
THE MACAWS, FOUND IN BRAZIL.

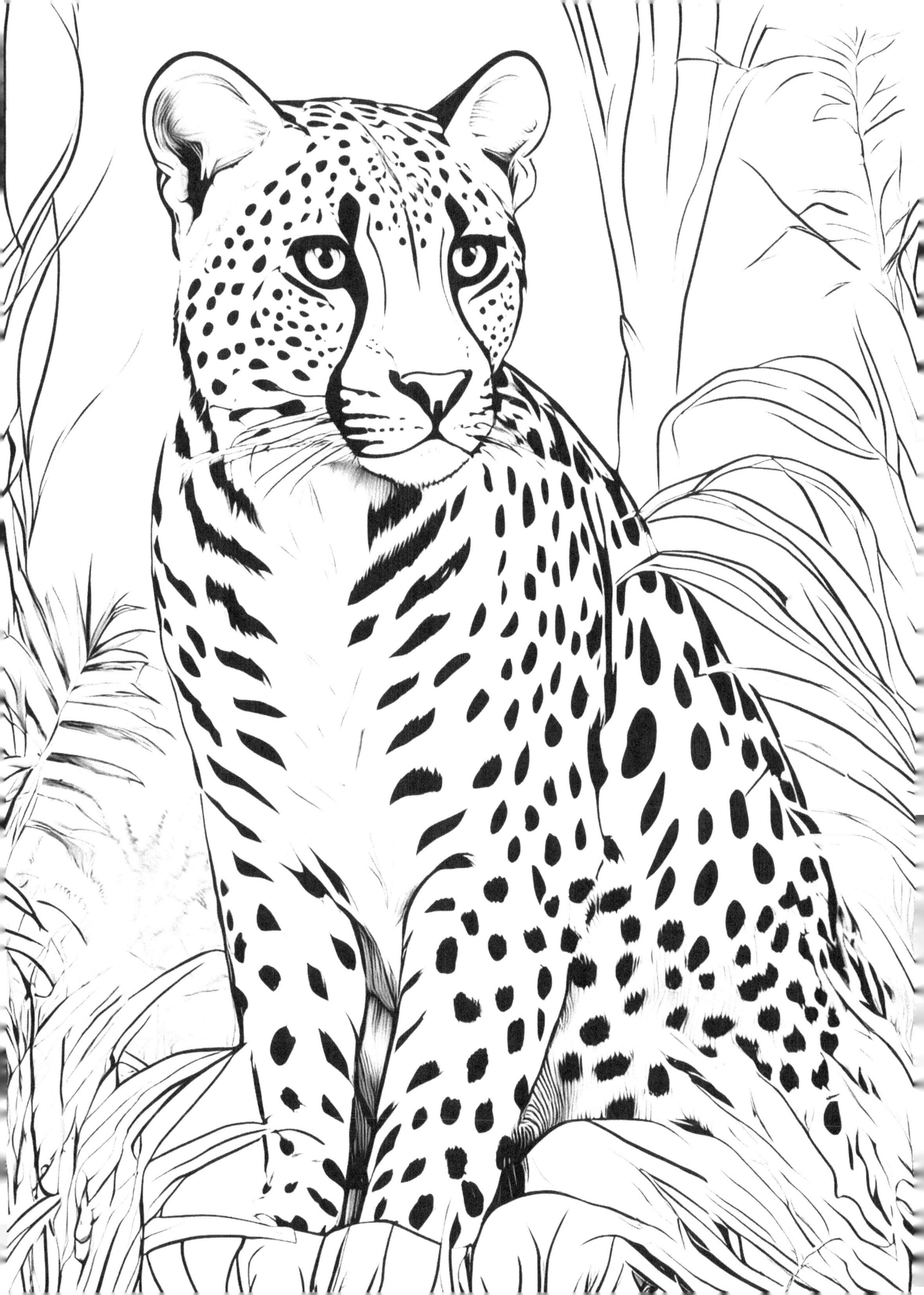

(ACINONYX JUBATUS VENATICUS) - CRITICALLY ENDANGERED, VERY
FEW REMAIN IN IRAN.

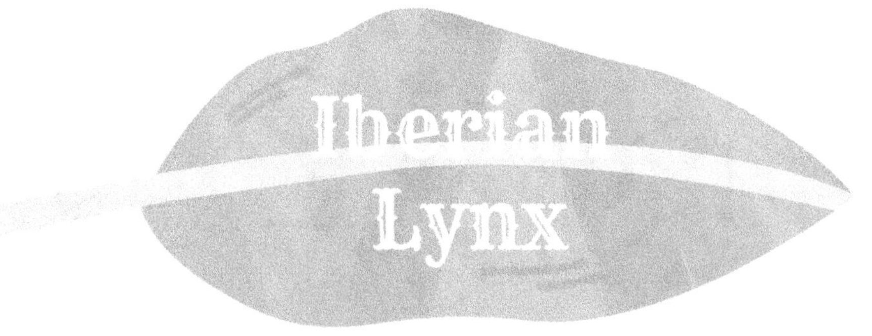

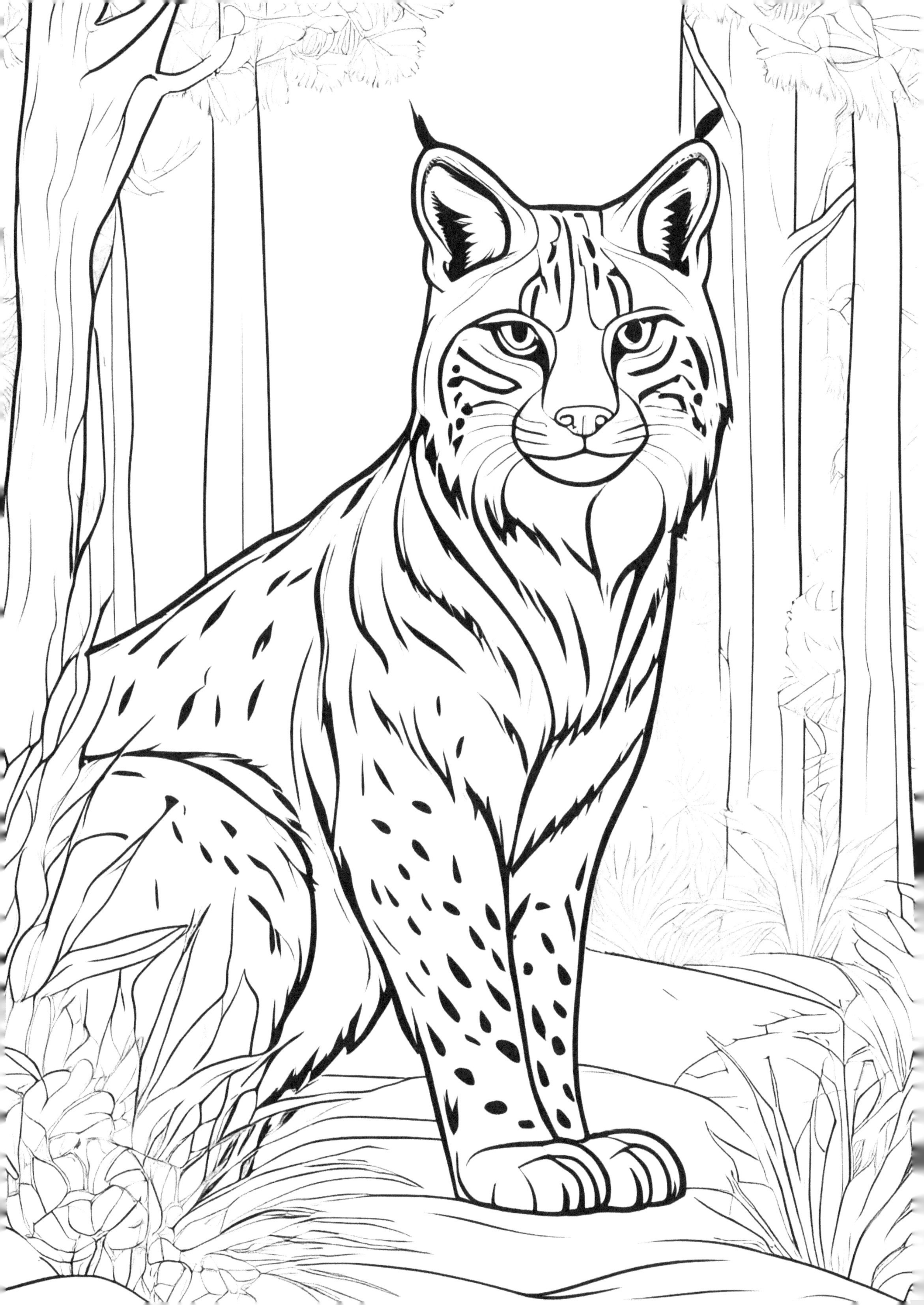

(LYNX PARDINUS) - A FELINE NATIVE TO THE IBERIAN
PENINSULA.

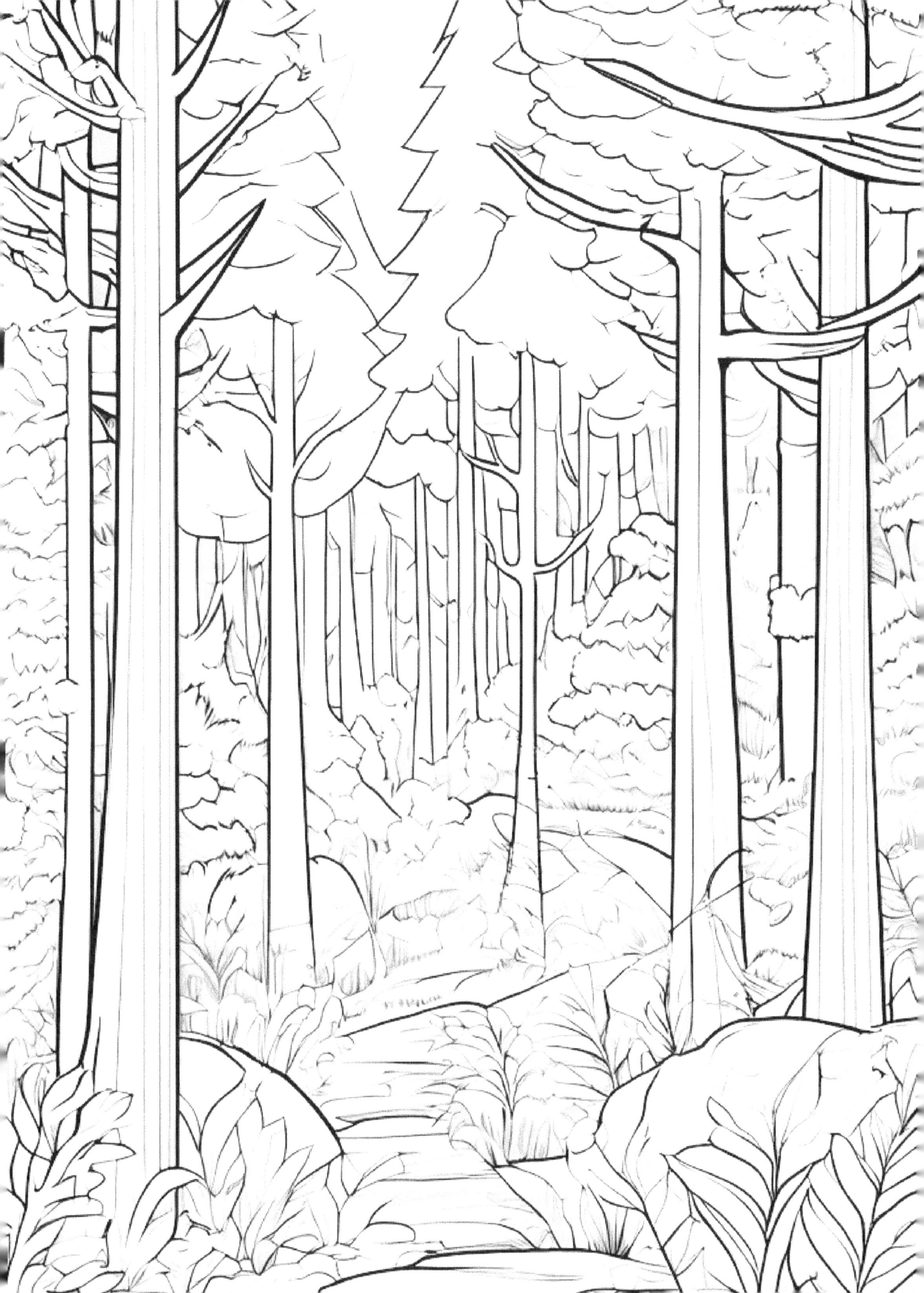